A VOICE FOR
EQUITY

BARBARA K. ROBERTS

NEWSAGE PRESS
Oregon

A Voice for Equity
Copyright © 2022 by Barbara K. Roberts

Paperback Original ISBN 978-0939165-81-0
Library Edition (Hardcover) ISBN 978-0939165-83-4
EPUB 978-0939165-82-7

NewSage Press
P.O. Box 610
Tillamook, OR 97141
503-695-2211

www.newsagepress.com

Cover & Book Design by Sherry Wachter
Printed in the United States
Distributed by Publishers Group West

Library of Congress Cataloging-in-Publication Data

Roberts, Barbara, 1936-
    A voice for equity / Barbara K. Roberts
        ISBN 978-0939165-81-0

DEDICATION

For the millions of Americans who have risked their reputations and their safety by speaking out on controversial social issues, by testifying before government bodies, and by marching and protesting to give greater visibility and strength to their messages.

Those brave voices won the right to vote for women in our country and still continue to fight for women's equality; saved and protected environmental treasures from sea to sea; fought for greater justice and fairness for all people of color and all nationalities; insist on equal treatment and access for people with disabilities; secured marriage rights and continue to expand respect for the LGBTQ community.

To all those caring voices, I salute your bravery, your conscience, your dedication, and the remarkable results you have brought to our nation. You all have my deepest gratitude.

CONTENTS

Acknowledgments . . . . *vi*
Foreword. . . . . *ix*

A VOICE FOR PEOPLE WITH DISABILITIES **1**
  1. A Future Governor Speaks Out for Disability Rights 3
  2. Answering the Call for the Children 13

A VOICE FOR WOMEN **19**
  3. Feminist Leadership: Making History .21
  4. Capturing Women's History: Telling the Stories. 29
  5. Looking Back, Moving Forward: NARAL Pro-Choice Oregon 37

A VOICE FOR OREGON **43**
  6. Naming Ceremony for Oregon's Human Services Building 45
  7. Why Are They Angry? Citizens & Their Government 49
  8. Portland State University Commencement Address 63
  9. Finding a Place: The Trials and Triumphs of the Displaced 69
  10. The Practice of Leadership and Change 85
  11. Climbing the Mountains of Change. .95
  12. Voting: Inclusion, Exclusion, Confusion 105

A VOICE FOR LGBTQ RIGHTS. **117**
Preface
  13. The Threat to LGBT Rights in Oregon 118
  14. Bringing It Home: Gay Youth, Families, and the LGBT Movement . .125
  15. Harvey Milk Foundation 131

A VOICE FOR DEATH WITH DIGNITY **135**
Preface
  16. American Academy of Bereavement Conference 137
  17. Association for Death Education & Counseling Conference 140
  18. Press Conference on Death with Dignity 143
  19. Compassion and Choices 147
  20. Testimony to Vermont Senate Health and Welfare Committee 151

A VOICE FOR THE ENVIRONMENT **157**
  21. Eleven-Year Retrospective of the Clinton Forest Plan 159
  22. Bureau of Land Management and the Public Lands 167

Author's Reflections *181*
About the Author *183*
The Barbara Roberts Collection, Portland State University *186*

ACKNOWLEDGMENTS

As I BEGAN SORTING through more than five hundred of my speeches, written and delivered over more than three decades, I turned for advice to the staff at Portland State University (PSU) library. After my retirement as Oregon's Governor, I donated boxes of my personal papers to the library's Special Collections Department that includes both written and video-taped speeches. From that initial library contact was born a special collaboration that resulted in plans for the publication of this book by NewSage Press, plus the video component of PSU's library creation, "Barbara Roberts Video Gallery." My special gratitude to Christine Paschild, head of PSU's Special Collection Department and their university archivist, and her amazing support staff—Carolee Harrison, Rhiannon Cates, Marti Clemmons, and Katrina Windon. Their talent and dedication created this unusual product.

As I began to edit and assemble this book, I found that my patience and many of my previous computer skills had disappeared. So, the data entry work to make this manuscript "publisher ready" fell to three dedicated friends: Gail Johnson, an author of a book on American women governors; Lisa Nelson, the talented and detail-oriented daughter of my partner Don Nelson; and Andrea Meyer, a long-time progressive political friend. These three women labored over copies of my original handwritten speeches that even included my original edits in pink ink! They helped with spelling, grammar, dates, and unfinished sentences— and they saved my mental health. My gratitude to these three women stretches far beyond this brief acknowledgement!

I also offer a special "Thank You" to my dear, longtime friend Terry Bean for his generosity and encouragement.

I extend my strongest gratitude to my publisher and editor Maureen R. Michelson of NewSage Press for stepping forward to create this book, which is our third publishing adventure. In 2002, NewSage Press joined me, a first-time author, in the publication of my first book, *Death without Denial: Grief without Apology.* Then in 2016, Maureen and I worked together again, revising and updating a second edition of *Death Without Denial.* I am so grateful to work with Maureen, once again, on a project we both believe in. Her final edits and book preparation have been invaluable. And NewSage Press's book designer, Sherry Wachter, has once again worked her designer magic to bring this book to life visually.

I treasure the support that my life partner, Don Nelson, has given me as I complete this book. He believes in my voice. He believes in me. I treasure that belief.

And finally, I thank you, my readers.

FOREWORD

I HAVE BEEN WRITING and delivering speeches and public presentations for decades. Early on, the speeches filled my need to voice my feelings on causes that mattered to me—children with disabilities, women's rights, environmental concerns. As time passed, I became actively involved in the political arena and my commitment to change expanded to outspoken presentations of advocacy, whether it was to support a particular candidate's campaign, my active support for gay rights, speaking for leadership with courage, or my work for Death with Dignity.

In 2002, I wrote a book on death and the importance of grieving, *Death Without Denial, Grief Without Apology*. My second book was my autobiography, *Up the Capitol Steps*, published in 2011. This was followed by a second edition of *Death Without Denial* in 2016, which specifically updated the progress made nationally for assisted dying.

My books have expanded my speaking opportunities and audiences, reaching people far beyond the political arena. The invitations to speak publicly have continued to flow over the years—from book readings, to keynote speeches at conferences and commencement addresses, to panels on women's leadership. I have given Rotary and Kiwanis luncheon addresses, and lectures in classrooms from Harvard to the University of Oregon.

And just when I began to think I had said it all, I recognized a pattern, perhaps even a "life focus" that had emerged. The passion that continues to move me is giving voice to—and advocating for—fairness, equality, a level playing field, decency, and dignity. My passion had a place and I realized that my voice mattered.

With this book, I have gathered a compilation of my messages of advocacy on a range of subjects. Space limitations necessitated careful editing, but I have worked to remain true to the messages as delivered over this thirty-three-year period.

In my 85th year, I still feel great passion for the topics I have championed in so many of my speeches. I hope my passion comes through, dear reader.

Please, sense my urgency of message.
Be open to making change.
BE THE VOICE.

—Governor Barbara Roberts
March 2022

Section One

A Voice for People with Disabilities

Barbara Roberts with her son Michael Sanders, two years old.

Speech One

A FUTURE GOVERNOR SPEAKS OUT FOR DISABILITY RIGHTS

Salem, Oregon — October 1990

Introduction: I begin this book with a speech I gave to a conference on disabilities organized by outgoing Governor Neil Goldschmidt in the fall of 1990. The subject of this speech reflects one of my earliest and most personally profound areas of advocacy—the rights of children with disabilities.

My work and support for my autistic son's right to a public education set the tone and the path I walked for the rest of my life. Michael was diagnosed with autism as a preschooler. When he was six years old in 1962, I enrolled him in public school, but I soon faced the harsh realities of rejection and unfairness when Mike was excluded from public school.

I began to use my anger, my frustration, and my voice to change the life of my older son and in the process, I changed my life as well.

Throughout this book, you will read references to my fight for Mike's right to be educated. It often comes up in my work and my words because this fight was the launching pad for both my career in elected politics and my role as a social advocate. My voice is never far from that consequential beginning.

Fifty years ago, when I was a child, severely handicapped and chronically ill children often times did not survive beyond early age. Thirty years ago, when my older son was a toddler, disabled children lived to adulthood in almost all cases—but that was about all they did. They didn't go to school, they didn't work, they didn't participate in athletics, recreation, or art. They were not part of their community. Many of them ended up in institutions.

I look back on that period and I can only think of it as "the dark ages"—dark ages for children with disabilities, dark ages for their parents.

I remember the darkness well because I was one of those parents. My older son, Mike, is autistic. Today, thousands of people in America have some new understanding of what autistic means. One of America's most successful movies last year, Rain Man, was the story of an autistic man. Autism finally stepped out of the closet as a disabling condition.

But I remember the pain of the dark ages.

I remember when Mike was sent home from public school in the first grade—not for the day—but forever.

I remember the diagnosis at University Medical School when Mike was six years old: "extremely emotionally disturbed." Recommendation: "Permanent institutionalization."

I remember the first time I heard the word "autism" applied to my son.

I remember the first time I described my son as autistic to an audience.

I remember the so-called "authority" on autism, Bruno Bettelheim, and that he declared the cause of autism was "refrigerator mothers."

I remember the three years Mike was in a private institution program and my weekly sessions with his caseworker. I never gave up that the caseworker was wrong: "Barbara, this is not like heart disease: nobody's going to discover a cure. If you want to help Mike, you have to understand that you are a major part of the cause."

And I remember a brand-new group called the National Society for Autistic Children. Back in the dark ages, this group gave parents our first advice and information about one of the most mystifying of diseases. They gave us knowledge and they gave us hope. They told us about research projects and medication possibilities and new books, and they held the first conferences on autism.

For most of us, such a fledgling organization became our first support group. There were no answers at your doctor's office, or your school district, or from your government. There were no answers at our little chapter meetings either—but neither were there the familiar questions:

– Why doesn't your little boy go to school?
– What's the matter with your child?
– You do understand, Barbara, why I'd rather Mike didn't play with my children?
– Do you really think it's fair to Mike to take him out in such public settings?
– Wouldn't it be better for everyone if you put Mike in a place where they know how to deal with children like him?

With support and accurate information from the National Society for Autistic Children, we were in a support group of parents who didn't ask the questions for which we had no answer. We had someone to talk to—someone to share with who was in the same boat, someone who understood.

With this group, a new door had opened and we stepped out of the closet of autism. We took our first steps, hesitantly, out of the dark ages.

And as parents, we discovered "out-of-the-closet" was a little like letting the genie out of the bottle. There's no turning back. Our children needed more, deserved more, had the right to more. Things can't grow or bloom in the closet because there is no light, but once we stepped out into the sunshine with our children, something blossomed—and that something was "advocacy."

The Oregon Chapter of the National Society for Autistic Children, a fledgling group in the Portland area in the early 1970s, had the audacity to come to the Oregon legislature and ask for public education for our children. There was no federal or state law, yet, this was in 1971 but we knew our children could benefit from special education and we felt as parents and taxpayers we had the right to expect public education for our children.

Our little group of parents had come together because our kids were fortunate enough to be in a short-term, federally-funded research project in the Parkrose School District. The federal government wanted to find out if "emotionally disturbed" children could be educated in the public-school setting. We began to see change, improvement, in our children.

Soon, we became parents unwilling to take our kids and go back in the closet. Our children were in school and we didn't intend to simply take them home when the federal project funds ran out, so we began to organize. We invited then State Representative Frank Roberts to one of our meetings and sought his help in introducing legislation. He agreed to help. Soon, we had a real piece of legislation, a bill, and printed right at the top, "introduced by Representative Frank Roberts at the request of the Oregon Chapter of the National Society for Autistic Children."

The bill would require public education for emotionally handicapped children in Oregon. It created a state advisory committee for emotionally handicapped children. And it created local advisory groups in school districts that participated and accepted any of the state funds.

Amazingly, part of the advisory committee membership had to be parents. Not only were we asking for education for our kids, not only were we asking for state funds, but we were going to advise the state and local education districts on their programs for emotionally handicapped children, for our children.

It's hard to imagine today, a time when parents of children with disabilities had so little of a role in determining their child's future. It was common to not share with parents the details of their child's diagnosis. "It's just as well you don't know all that technical stuff—it would just confuse and upset you."

In many cases, the only way the state was willing to pay for the expensive care for my child in a private institutional setting was if I signed my parental rights over to the state. I had three choices; to pay a monthly cost that was more than our monthly family income, to sign the papers, or to remove my child from the only facility in Oregon—private or public—that was giving treatment to autistic children.

It's difficult to imagine a time with no support groups, no advocacy groups, no doctors or special education teachers who could help—not even any lawyers who could plead your case, because there was no law on your side, or any laws at all. Not only could you not have your day in the sunshine, you couldn't have your day in court.

Those things are hard to imagine today.

Yet, twenty years ago, the other thing that was hard to imagine was advocacy for those with disabilities. But advocate we did. Our small group of parents started a speakers' bureau. We talked to Kiwanis and Rotary and anyone who would listen. We met more often and we planned more. Our group added new members and supporters. We opened a little bank account. We wrote letters. We wrote to the newspapers and to legislators. And we got ready to lobby our legislative proposal in Salem.

State Representative Frank Roberts, our legislative advocate, warned us to be realistic. This was a new idea. Our first and most difficult job would be educating legislators. Our chances of success in the 1971 session were slim. "Sometimes," he said, "a new idea takes several sessions to pass in the legislature—especially funding measures."

I agreed to become our group's part-time lobbyist. I was recently divorced and I was raising my two sons alone without child support. I was working full time at fairly low wages, but I took every Friday off and spent it in Salem lobbying for our special bill. I couldn't afford it, but it was too dark in the closet of autism and I couldn't go back, so I became a lobbyist.

Imagine again with me—this parent—young, politically unsophisticated, walking up the marble steps of our state capitol with one goal in mind: To change the world for our children with disabilities.

I had no experience. I was so scared. Plus, I couldn't afford to buy even a cup of coffee for a senator or representative. I didn't even know where the women's restroom was. But I was determined, I was committed, I knew our cause was right. The rest I could learn. And I did.

I learned that the Oregon legislative system was a very open one. I learned very quickly that legislators were real people. I found it was OK to be emotional about our cause. The system was more than just facts and figures. I found that a legislator would take your cause to other legislators, and I found that paid, professional, seasoned lobbyists would give you some pointers, even if you were green and lost.

So, I worked for five months as a lobbyist. I talked to every senator and every representative. Our group wrote letters and called legislators. And I talked the Senate Education Committee into holding a rare, night hearing. That evening, thirty people came to support our legislation. One of those people was my young son Mike. He had written his own testimony and wanted to share with the committee how wonderful it was to be in the experimental classes, in school with other children, how much he was learning, and how other kids were learning about him, and his handicap. Kids stopped making fun of him in school. Mike told the committee that for him, special education was not special. "For me," he said, "it's all there is."

The committee was fascinated; some of the senators were misty-eyed. The bill passed the committee unanimously and it passed the senate unanimously. And the Ways and Means Committee put $50,000 into the first funding for the bill. Every member of the Oregon House of Representatives, except one, voted for our bill. (One representative was in the men's room.)

We had done it. Even with the two, full-time professional lobbyists from the Oregon School Boards Association working against our bill, we had done it. We understood that the mountain of government was movable. We had moved the mountain. I had personally learned that one person could make a difference. By the end of that legislative session, I had new credentials as a citizen lobbyist, and a new man in my life, Frank Roberts.

Our parents' group had a real first success! But I don't want to mislead you that the theme music comes up here, the credits start rolling on the screen and we are pictured walking into the sunset, hand-in-hand, with our children.

It wasn't quite that simple.

That 1971 law made some funds available. It encouraged education for some of our children, but it took years more to have the programs in place, special education teachers trained and hired, lawsuits won, more legislative battles fought, passage of the federal law, funding fights, school-board battles, and advocacy, advocacy, and more advocacy!

I look back to when the U.S. Congress passed Public Law 94-142, Education for All Handicapped Children Act, in 1975 that required education for all our children, and many of our hopes were answered. It meant that our children had rights. We often had to advocate for those rights in courtrooms and in the school-board rooms, but at least we had the law on our side. The federal government has never kept its promise on the percentage of funding it would provide to each state, but handicapped children clearly have education rights under both Oregon and federal law.

So finally, someone could start composing the theme music for the educational part of our story!

A few years later, new scripts were being written. A new generation came along to advocate for expanded services for those with disabilities. All too soon, our children grew to adulthood. Those of us who worked on the education efforts in the 1970s began advocating for other needs for disabled adults—employment, group living situations, community support services, transportation, job training.

We will never again sit silently by and allow our society to put our children, at any age, back in the closet.

Susan B. Anthony, leader of the women's suffrage movement in America, made a very short but significant statement about advocacy over 100 years ago. I think it is a slogan we could easily adopt: "Never another season of silence."

How important our voices are! And what a chorus they have become—parents, teachers, siblings, employers, educational groups, strong support organizations, and disabled citizens themselves—speaking out, advocating, changing the world.

Today, no single parent walks up the state capitol steps as a single voice for our concerns. Now, strong organizations advocate, lobby, and serve disabled citizens.

After thirty years of speaking out as an advocate for the handicapped and disabled, fighting for their education, employment, access to public transit, telephone systems for the deaf, retraining of injured workers, recreational opportunities, sponsoring the legislation that created the Oregon Disabilities Commission, I thought I understood. I thought I was sensitive. I thought I was aware. And then my husband, Frank Roberts, was diagnosed with cancer in the summer of 1987. Radiation treatment killed the nerves in his legs and put him permanently in a wheelchair, and I began a whole new process of education by crisis.

We've learned to check out restaurant accessibility before we go someplace to eat. We travel quite a bit and finding truly accessible motels and hotels are rare and in limited supply. We've learned to make reservations—and make them early. One hundred rooms in a hotel with one or two accessible, is not unusual and it's almost never a view room! Even with a handicapped parking permit, parking is a constant headache, and I'm getting seriously aggressive about able-bodied people who "steal" handicapped parking spots.

We can no longer accept just any invitation we get. Half of them, at least, are not wheelchair accessible. And when you ask first, the information is, as often as not, wrong. Theatres, restrooms, airplanes, hotels, shopping centers, even school building, have architectural barriers and attitudinal barriers.

Now, Frank and I are much better-informed advocates than we were two years ago. We are sharing our new knowledge with the Oregon legislature, with local governments, and with the public. We hope our new knowledge will be recognized as much more than self-interest as we advocate for necessary changes. The advocacy must go on; the work must continue.

When we brought children with disabilities into our elementary and highs schools, there would never be a turning back. Education and training needs, and desires have moved on to our community colleges, our universities, and our law schools. From there, we will see changes to our office buildings, work sites, courtrooms, and our legislative systems. In this 1990 election, my husband is running for re-election. He may be the first Oregon legislative candidate to run for office from a wheelchair. He can't go door to door in his political campaign, so he is working on creative ways to reach his voters in their neighborhoods.

So, as you participate in this historic conference, set a strong, but realistic legislative agenda. You won't see legislation of the magnitude of the new Americans with Disabilities Act enacted every year, but every year must be a year of gain for Oregonians with disabilities.

I look forward to seeing the product of this conference. I look forward to adding my support to your legislative package.

I look forward to signing your bills into law as Oregon's new governor.

"Never another season of silence!"

A participant in the "Youth Games" sponsored by Special Olympics Oregon. Governor Roberts has supported Special Olympics for many years and has served as a board member.

Speech Two

ANSWERING THE CALL
FOR THE CHILDREN

Portland, Oregon — September 2004

Introduction: I have spent tremendous amounts of time in my life engaged in activities and organizations benefitting children, whether it was school-board service, child abuse prevention, services for children with disabilities, advocacy for special education, Girl Scouts, or Special Olympics.

In 2004, I received an invitation to speak at a luncheon co-sponsored by the Oregon Alliance of Children's Programs and Ecumenical Ministries of Oregon. These two groups are seldom found co-sponsoring a program, so it immediately piqued my interest. As I carefully read the letter of invitation, a single paragraph captured my decision to say "yes":

"It is easy for many of us to feel discouraged these days. We are looking for inspiration. Your personal story advocating for children and running for public office is important.... How can us 'regular folks' be involved in public policy?"

These words from Allen Hunt, Executive Director of William Temple House, Episcopal Mission Society, had not only swayed me, but had also offered me a passionate speaking challenge before a diverse audience of advocates for children and families.

"Regular folks" they called themselves, with a mission of collaboration and kindness. Believe me, there is nothing regular about that. They asked me to "rally the troops" as the election season approached and the legislative session neared. Their timing was well thought out. I was eager to answer their call!

⌒⟶

Well, this is a day to celebrate! The Oregon Alliance for Children's Programs and the Ecumenical Ministries coming together—professionals and volunteers from many of our most significant child and family agencies, and our community's faith-based organizations. This represents one of the things I love best—*collaborating* with *kindness!*

When Coleen Lewis and Allen Hunt ganged up on me, telling me about their vision for today's program, I'd intended to say, "No." My September calendar was full to overflowing and I thought, *No more space!*

But mention collaboration and kids in the same breath, and I'm hooked! So, here I am.

As I thought about what I wanted to say to you today, I was struck by the "glowing introductions" I often receive on days like this one, and how *far removed* a former governor can seem to be from the audiences we speak to. So, I thought it might be useful for you to learn a few things about me that never get told when I'm introduced.

First of all, I am one of the most *unlikely* persons to become a governor that you are ever likely to meet. I grew up in a very small town in Oregon. My family was totally blue collar. And growing up in the 1940s and 1950s in small-town Oregon meant I had no women role models for the person I later became. Small-town high schools of the 1950s produced no female athletes and no female student body presidents.

I was a good student, salutatorian of my high school graduating class, editor of the school paper, secretary of the student body, active in class plays and chorus, a cheerleader, and president of our school service club. Yet, no one ever suggested I go to college—not a teacher, a parent, a class advisor. *No one.*

I married in the middle of my senior year, graduated in June 1955 and spent the next three years in Texas as a military wife. By the time I turned 21, I had two sons. Not anyone would call my early life a recommended *career path* to become governor! Yet today, I feel strongly that too many Americans, too many Oregonians, are watching from the sidelines, unwilling, or uncomfortable with becoming participants in the political process.

So, when I say that, I sometimes watch the expressions in an audience and I can see the *look*: The *look* means, "Easy for you to say. You've been the governor."

Well, lest you believe that I and other governors are some kind of a unique and special breed, let me assure you that we are not unlike millions of other citizens (just like you) across the nation. And as I've said hundreds of times, each of you is only one cause, one concern, one tragedy, one moral indignation away from active political involvement. The cause that stirs you, may be just around the corner. It may be in this room.

I began my political career as a citizen advocate, a parent, seeking educational rights for my autistic son, who had been sent home from school in the first grade—not for the day, but forever. His handicap meant he had no right to a public-school education.

However, I simply could not accept the unfairness, the inequity. I spoke out publicly about this injustice. I pleaded for help. I waited for a leader to step forward to champion our autistic children's causes.

By the end of the 1960s, I was a divorced mother with two sons, no child support, and a low-paying office job, but I was no longer willing to let those liabilities short-change my son. I finally came to recognize I had two crucial assets—a cause and a mother's anger!

So, I took a day a week off work (and the painful related pay cut), traveled to our state capitol building and began a fight for my son's educational rights. I was politically inexperienced and scared to death. Yet, I marched up the capitol steps determined to change the world for the disabled children of our state. Five months later, Oregon had the first such special education rights law in the nation—five years before the federal law for special education rights had passed.

That first political success for my son cemented my belief that if your cause is just, and you are determined enough, and if you can make your case well, one person can make a difference in the political process. I learned it then. I believe it still.

Sometimes when searching for a leader, we discover the leadership within ourselves. You can see why I believe in citizen participation. You can understand why I preach that democracy is not a spectator sport. One committed person can indeed make a difference.

However, I do know that to those who have not experienced the political system "up-close and personal," it can look pretty daunting and complicated. But it is like any other skill—it can be learned, even mastered. You start with the easy stuff.

First, learn the names of your city council members, county commissioners, your own state senator, and your own state representative. That's only twelve names—a dozen folks. Then learn the names of your five statewide elected officeholders; the governor, secretary of state, attorney general, state treasurer, and commissioner of Labor and Industries. Now, we're up to seventeen names. For this *first* challenge you only have three more names; your two U.S. senators and your own U.S. congressperson. That is twenty names, total.

Every classroom teacher in Oregon has learned almost twice as many student names when her new class arrived this fall. I'll bet you can easily name twenty entertainers or sports figures, and they have a whole lot less impact on your life than the twenty people whose names can begin to make you politically literate.

While "politically literate" is important, even more important is earning a good grade in citizenship.

In order to become an "A" citizen you must take the most crucial first step—*register to vote.* And because this is an election year, you will need to be registered by October 12. If you miss that step, you won't have a voice in this fall's election for president, on ballot measures, or to choose your state legislator or mayor.

So, continuing to work toward your "A" in citizenship, volunteer to help the candidates of your choice by putting up their lawn sign in your yard, taking brochures door-to-door, or showing off their bumper sticker on your car.

Those lessons are an important part of the picture, however, I'd like to take a couple of minutes to explain another kind of picture.

After I left office as Governor, I had time to really reflect on the experience I'd had as a public leader, and I came to realize something that I had never quite recognized in the middle of the fray of being governor. Each office holder plays their role as a leader in front of the backdrop of their times. It is much like the old vaudeville theatre where each act is performed before the painted backdrop of a city scene, or a riverboat dock, a farm scape. Well, leaders do much the same thing, but the backdrop may not be one of their choosing or one that they've created.

My backdrops as Governor included the huge challenge of newly passed Measure 5, the massive controversy of the spotted owl/timber crisis, three attempts to recall me from office, and the fastest growing Oregon population since the wagon trains arrived on the Oregon Trail. Tough issues. Challenging backdrops—not of my making but on my platter. That's the way backdrops work.

So, we all must do the work we do for children and families with the backdrops that are part of today's financial and political reality for Oregon. We must not waste our time or energies lamenting the way it *should* be or the way we *wish* it were. We will work long-term for those changes, but we must now be the best-prepared advocates for our children and families—the hardest working, most committed advocates we can be.

We face poverty, hunger, a health care crisis, educational cuts, and housing issues, *all* set against the backdrop of state and local budgets facing ongoing stress and increasing shortfalls. We can't be afraid or unwilling to make our voices heard in the political process. And we cannot shy away from the legislature just because we don't feel politically sophisticated enough to make our case. If not us, then who?

For example, I'm currently serving on the Governor's Health Policy Commission and I'll be in Salem working for prescription benefits, healthcare access, and children's health insurance. I've been a member of the Children's Relief Nursery Board in St. Johns for five years and I'll be in the Capitol advocating for funding for these children (birth to three years) who are victims of child abuse and neglect. I refuse to let them become *prison fodder* down the road.

It is not a matter of my political sophistication; it is a matter of my passion for children. I speak out in the legislature, in local government settings, in the voters' pamphlet, in the newspaper, and in other public settings because I still believe that one person can make a difference.

It's *not* because I'm a former governor—it's because I'm a *current* citizen. And when I get tempted to back away from my commitment and believe it's someone else's turn—I remember my son Mike, and I accept another chance to speak; I write another fundraising letter for a cause I believe in; I walk a few more miles for AIDS, or peace, or heart disease, or equality; I host another candidate fundraiser; I write another letter to the editor.

And I remember my favorite quote from my inaugural address: "Each generation has but one chance to be judged by future generations, and this is our time."

Never let it be said that we fell short of commitment or passion when we had the chance to make a difference for those in need.

Let's not settle for anything less than an "A" for good citizenship—an "A" for children.

Section Two

A Voice
for Women

Speech Three

FEMINIST LEADERSHIP: MAKING HISTORY

Portland, Oregon — October 2003

Introduction: I delivered the keynote speech for the First Annual Oregon National Organization of Women (NOW) Awards Brunch held in downtown Portland. The theme for the event was "Feminism Now and Tomorrow." More than 300 women attended the lovely brunch, including several state-elected women, all of them enthusiastic for the cause.

The gathering was held at a large popular hotel and it definitely was a step up from the smaller, more familiar wine-and-cheese receptions so often held for these women's gatherings in the past. The audience seemed in high spirits and perhaps, ready for a little "raised fist" action. This was a perfect audience for my message of feminist leadership.

WE WERE ALL BORN IN THE 20TH CENTURY, and as females from that century, we have been privileged to live in the most historic century of women's progress *ever.* Never take for granted what you have witnessed and the role you have played as that history unfolds before your very eyes.

For, in fact, part of what we have done, and are continuing to do at this point in history, is "carry the water" for generations of women who will follow us. The truth is, for most women in this country, someone else carried *our* water…and we can't afford to *return an empty bucket.* Women marched and were *jailed,* and were spat upon, and even force fed just so women could vote. So, *we* could vote.

Someone was the *first* woman in law school, the *first* female physician, the *first* woman professor, police officer, engineer, labor leader. *Someone* in this country was the first *and only* woman mayor, the first woman on a corporate board, the first woman to become a military officer, a college president, an astronaut, a councilwoman, a legislator, a judge—the list goes on. Across this country they carried *our* water.

And while history may not always measure these women fairly in terms of their accomplishments and leadership, they broke the molds and made it easier for the women who followed. That's what pathbreaking is all about. The women before us carried *our* water. They blazed the trails, and now we must *lay the concrete* for the women and girls who will follow.

Yet, today's luncheon theme, "Feminism Now and Tomorrow," may be slightly putting the cart before the horse without recognizing, acknowledging, and appreciating earlier feminist leadership and sacrifice that today allows us to march proudly into that future. These last thirty years, especially, have been about new pioneers and pathbreakers, about role models and risk-takers. We have been slowly educating this country to the capability, intelligence, skills, endurance, strength, and perseverance of women leaders in every part of this nation and in every field. And that has been particularly true in elective politics. But what was it that stirred so many women to run for office after decades, even centuries of being willing to accept *all-male* political leadership in this country? Well, academic researchers can speak volumes on that subject, but as a political practitioner, this is my theory:

Hundreds of thousands of women fought in every state in this nation to simply have our U.S. Constitution include *both* genders in the wording of its text, to put the words of the Equal Rights Amendment in our national document. Then, we watched the massive fight to *deny* that verbal equality. As a result, women became more politicized by the *failure* of the ERA than they might have become with its *passage*. When women were denied a place in the Constitution, they ran for public office and *won* the places in state legislative assemblies, city councils, congressional seats, and finally, governors' chairs. And now, that trend has become an unstoppable river.

Across this country women are no longer willing to step aside, allowing others to make decisions for their children, for their health choices, for their communities, their state, and their future. Women are in decision-making roles in this country at every level of government—school boards, local government, state assemblies, Congress, and our judicial benches. We have witnessed a *political revolution:* We are at the table and we are changing the menu.

But we should not celebrate these gains without recognizing the sacrifices others made—the cost of women's political victories.

In Oregon, for instance, I watched two viable, capable women run for governor and lose. Two women ran for the U.S. Senate and lost. A woman who was one-hundred-percent qualified ran for Oregon state treasurer and lost. Women in Oregon ran for U.S. Congress and lost. But one painful brick after another, these women paved the path that helped me and other women *win.* In Oregon, we have now had a female U.S. Senator, three women in Congress, two women superintendents of public instruction in Oregon, two female secretaries of state, three women on our state supreme court, three women mayors of Portland, four women speakers of the house, two women on our federal bench, and I have served as Oregon's governor. More and more bricks—successes—pave a longer and longer path for other women to follow. And before you know it, it is no longer simply a path, but it is a solid foundation on which new women leaders may stand tall.

Today, our obligations and responsibilities, our opportunities and options, lay before us, much like the vast lands that faced the pioneer women who walked across this country to settle the

American West. This is the chance to lead that we've worked for, prepared for, and sometimes, even demanded.

Looking historically at the most recent national picture, from 1974 when Ella Grasso was elected Governor of Connecticut, until 2002 when, for the first time in American history, four women were elected governor on the same night, the political climate is *clearly* changing.

In November 2002, the elections of Jennifer Granholm, Democrat of Michigan; Linda Lingle, Republican of Hawaii; Janet Napolitano, Democrat of Arizona; and Kathleen Sebelius, Democrat of Kansas, brought to seventeen the number of female governors elected "in their own right." In a quarter of a century, we have changed the face of American politics. It is now impossible to put "Jeanie" back in the bottle. It is not just our *history*—it is our *future*.

And I can't tell you what a privilege and honor it's been for me to be part of making some of that history—laying some of that concrete for our foundation. Yet, even after a decade, I still find myself at a loss for words when I attempt to describe what it was like to serve as governor of our state. It was part hot seat and part spotlight.

I have lots of scar tissue from my times in the hot seat, but also lots of wonderful memories from my times in the spotlight. And I must confess, the spotlight can be fun and occasionally, a nice salve for one's ego. I loved being the commander-in-chief of our state's National Guard! I adored four years of never needing to search for a parking spot. And I never tired of being introduced as Oregon's first woman governor!

But those fun times were offset dramatically by facing the grieving families of the forest fire jumpers from Oregon who died in Colorado in 1994; and by dealing with my first experience walking the length of death row in the state penitentiary and seeing the faces of the eleven men behind those metal bars. Those sad memories will be with me for a long time.

Yet, if I had to choose one of the most unique personal experiences relating to my tenure as governor, it was one that actually took place two years *after* I left office—the unveiling of my official governor's portrait; talk about feeling like an historical artifact! Yet, it feels very strange to know that the portrait will be hanging in the Oregon State Capitol long after I'm gone, and school children will hear about how I was the *first* woman Governor of Oregon. Hopefully, by then, they'll think, *"Why was that ever a big deal?"*

But today in 2003, it is *still* a big deal. And part of the reason is the extra difficulty women have in being accepted and recognized as leaders. Let me give you an example of the extra challenge women face in being seen as leaders. At this time in history, women are not perceived to be leaders—no matter *what* they accomplish or how well they do it. Our cultural yardstick for measuring leadership is clearly a white male measuring device!

Shortly after I was elected Governor, a news article in the *Oregonian* described my political career as a "sudden rise" to the governor's chair. Let me describe that "sudden rise" to you:

- Over thirty years of leadership on nonprofit boards.
- Forty years as a community activist.
- Secretary of the Oregon Democratic Party.
- Successful legislative advocate for disabled children.
- Ten years as an elected school board member.
- Four years as an elected community college board member.
- One year as an appointed county commissioner to fill a vacancy in the most populous county in the state.
- Four years as a state representative.
- Two years as the first woman house majority leader.
- Six years as elected secretary of state (also filling the roles as lieutenant governor and state auditor).
  - Became first Democratic secretary of state in 114 years. I won all 36 counties in my 1988 re-election.

"A sudden rise" to the governor's chair? I think not!
A male political figure who had moved up through the

ranks—as I did—would be seen as a leader long before they arrived in the governor's office. We just don't *look* like leaders are supposed to look. They simply couldn't *see me coming.*

Now, my intention is not to whine about this issue, as frustrating as it is, but to help each of you, each of *us,* understand the reality of that cultural measuring stick and to recognize that as nontraditional leaders, as "path-breakers," women must continue to lead effectively with or without the recognition. That is the role of pioneers.

Over the decades, women have stepped forward to save parts of the environment, to raise awareness of breast cancer and AIDS, to clamp down on drunk driving and gun violence. Women leaders, working on equal pay for women, on health care for children, on affordable housing, childcare, and senior citizen services can be found in *every* state in this nation.

Yet, if we know our history, we will find that our foremothers had been treading this path long before us. The women of 100 years ago were fighting for child labor laws, the right to family planning information, college entrance for women students, inheritance rights and property rights for women, and to end racial segregation. Women's passion and commitment *and leadership* on so many crucial social issues have made America a better place—decade after decade after decade.

And this is no time for women to step away from that leadership *or* that history. Nor should we step away from the label of today's program—*feminist.*

I tell people around the country that I ran as a pro-choice, pro-environment, pro-gay, civil libertarian, *feminist* Democrat—and *WON!*

We should not *flinch* or *step away* from our feminist label. It represents equality, fairness, acceptance, vigilance, equity, and higher expectations for our society. We should wear the title with pride. The future of America may well rest with the growing leadership of our nation's women—the environment, education, economy, healthcare, the arts, childcare, our legal systems, our community, "quality of life," decent housing, and

safe schools. Our leadership in every facet of American life—
our voices, our impact—will put a brand on the nation our
children and grandchildren will inherit.

So, let me close with one brief story. When I served as
Oregon's secretary of state, I introduced a piece of legislation
to change Oregon's state motto *back* to our original territorial
motto. We translated the territorial motto from Latin to English
and then successfully passed the legislation.

Today, Oregon's state motto once again reflects my belief in
our *history* as women and our *destiny* as leaders.

As my state of Oregon pin says proudly: "She flies with her
own wings."

BARBARA ROBERTS FAMILY COLLECTION

State Capitol portrait of Governor Barbara Hughey Roberts
with Governor Roberts's granddaughter, Kaitlin Sanders,
standing in front of her grandmother's portrait in 1999.
The official gubernatorial portrait was painted by
Aimee Erickson in 1997.

ANDREA LONIS

Girl Scouts of Oregon and Southwest Washington present its annual Marie Lamfrom Women of Distinction awards to honor women's courageous leadership and role modeling for girls. A group photo at the 2019 awards included past and current honorees:

(from left) former chancellor, university president, and education leader Melody Rose, Ph.D., Attorney General Ellen Rosenblum, Oregon Supreme Court Justice Adrienne Nelson, Governor Barbara Roberts, retired Portland State University professor and community leader Barbara Alberty, Portland Police Chief Danielle Outlaw, Executive Director of Latino Network Carmen Rubio, and media consultants and business owners Victoria Lara and DJ Wilson.

Speech Four
CAPTURING WOMEN'S HISTORY: TELLING THE STORIES
Portland, Oregon — April 2012

Introduction: At a time in the United States when television, cell phones, computers, and iPads began providing a large share of the information our citizens consume, a thoughtful, innovative, broad-based organization began offering online talks in 2006. Called TED Talks (Technology, Education, Design), it focuses on international thinkers, leaders, and teachers for global audiences. This was later followed with TEDx talks, which features leading local voices from thousands of communities.

Invited TEDx speakers present their talks, which last about eighteen minutes, in auditoriums across the nation, addressing a wide range of topics. Those diverse topics have included juggling, car repair, history, futuristic travel, hip hop, healthcare, and so much more. Thousands of those presentations have been put online over the years and people worldwide have watched, learned, laughed, and cried. TEDx presentations inspire conversations in communities and often lead to changes in perspectives. I have always found them interesting and valuable, so to become a TEDx presenter was an honor.

In early spring 2012, I was invited to present a TEDx talk at Concordia University in Portland. Everything was planned like clock-work, including a get-acquainted social gathering beforehand with other presenters for that same day. The TEDx staff clarified presenters' topics and timed them. There was even a rehearsal day where the organizers coordinated a cue-to-cue production for each presenter. It was unlike any speaking experience I was accustomed to. I was impressed.

The topic of my TEDx presentation was women's history with two major focuses: the importance of preserving the history of women political pioneers and the unique histories of America's female governors. My presentation was posted online in 2012.

As of 2021, TEDx talks have now collectively received more than one billion hits, which translates into billions of listeners. Here is my contribution to that online record.

SOMETIMES I LAUGHINGLY REFER TO MYSELF as an *historical artifact!* After all, twenty years ago I was Oregon's first woman governor.

My portrait hangs in Oregon's State Capitol. I have some *things* named after me. But when all is said and done—*who cares?* We seldom read the names on government buildings. And when, if ever, was the last time most people visited their state capitol and perused the portraits of old governors? Not on most of our "to-do lists."

But that said, I find myself currently immersed in a period of historical reflection. This year, 2012, the state of Oregon is celebrating the *100th* anniversary of the passage of the ballot measure that gave Oregon women their voting rights. It had taken more than four decades of effort and five earlier ballot measure *defeats* to finally gain this success.

In 1912, Oregon women joined the women of Wyoming, Colorado, Utah, Idaho, and the state of Washington in securing their right to vote. The women of these six Western states were the first in the nation to secure voting rights when the *men* of their six states voted to extend suffrage to these Western women.

As my state has focused on this historical celebration, new research of this period is being funded; museums and libraries have displays of photographs, old newspapers, and historic campaign materials; re-enactments of voting debates are being presented on community stages across the state.

It has been fun and exciting to relive this very combative history. I have learned so much since this celebration began. And I have gained a new *commitment* to preserving this history—and to sharing it with broader audiences. History is meant *not* to sit on a shelf collecting dust, but to devour, think about, talk about, and share.

My state, for instance, has a unique collection of "first-hand" accounts of a huge piece of the history of the Western states. The Oregon Trail pioneers who traveled across this continent on the *trails west,* were uprooted from the East and Midwest, leaving behind everything they had known to venture into new territory and an unknown new life. That amazing six-month trek, long and difficult, was *captured* in hundreds of diaries written almost entirely by the women and teenage girls of those wagon trains.

They recorded the challenges, the births, the deaths, the changing landscapes, the hardships, and the hopes. They preserved the history of that massive migration west for all the generations that followed. First-hand accounts have an ability to not only record history, not only teach and educate, but to *transport* the reader back to another time, another place, another experience.

I personally never looked at those diaries without feeling the experience of my great-great-grandparents, James and Almeda Boggs, who, with their three children, came west on the Oregon Trail in 1853. They buried a daughter beside the trail. I have walked on the land they farmed. I have stood before their double headstone in a pioneer cemetery in Southern Oregon. *History* does not *sit on a shelf* when it becomes *family.*

It is in that vein that I took on a project of personal importance and Oregon historical significance. Almost six years ago, I undertook an effort that only a few elected women in our country have completed. I decided to write an autobiography— one that included my four years as Oregon governor.

At that time, Governor Madeleine Kunin of Vermont was the only female governor in our country to have put her life story in writing. Her book, *Living a Political Life,* was published in 1994. A decade later, no other woman governor had completed her autobiography. Governor Ann Richards of Texas had written her life story late in her term as state treasurer, but unfortunately that book preceded her experiences as a woman governor.

As one of America's first ten female governors, I was becoming alarmed that our place in history would go unrecorded, or told, perhaps by others, but not *by* the women who *politically pioneered* those offices.

Four of the first 10 women governors elected *in their own right* are already deceased. This unique set of stories of these early women political leaders were slipping through our fingers. This history needed to be told. Firsthand accounts can help a reader see the path—the path that takes a little girl from dolls and tea sets to the office of governor.

Like the writers of the Oregon Trail diaries, the history of these *political trailblazers* needs to be captured for the future. I began to feel a need, an obligation, to tell my story, to share a piece-of-the puzzle that helps complete the picture of America's early women governors.

I started this huge writing project with the idea this book could be a cinch. After all, I was there for every day of my life. All I had to do was put it on paper! Well, *surprise!* After more than five years' work, I recognized I had been traveling an emotional road, *unpacking* the boxes of my life. I had become part storyteller, part self-therapist.

I pushed my memory bank to the limits. My memories became a manuscript. I read biographies, autobiographies. I researched newspapers, the Oregon Archives state records, legislative papers, school records, family documents. My research began to create a piece of Oregon *historical documentation.*

I sorted through hundreds of photographs looking for images that would help tell the story of a small-town girl who became her state's first woman governor. I interviewed friends, family, colleagues, and former staff, verifying my own memories and adding some stories and color to my own recollections.

The project felt absolutely endless. As the years passed, it felt even more endless. But the ever-increasing page count and slowly added chapters gave me hope that a *real book* was in the making.

Finally, we were in the editing stage—my least favorite part of this lengthy project. Lots of give-and-take was required, especially when my editor *slashed* paragraphs that I knew were my "pearls of wisdom." Yet, I knew I had to decide when to let go and when to stand and fight for stories that I believed were essential to the book and to my story. At last, we were making the final decisions on the cover photo and the title for my book, *Up the Capitol Steps.*

By the time my autobiography was released in October 2011, it joined not only Governor Kunin's book but the autobiography of Governor Sarah Palin of Alaska. And in 2012, Governor Jennifer Granholm of Michigan released her fascinating political memoir from the years as her state's governor as she led the fight to bring Michigan back from the huge crisis of the auto industry crash.

Now, certainly this is a small number of stories to record the history of some of this nation's most notable women political pioneers. But perhaps we have started a trend that will encourage other women leaders to record their story—to inspire, teach, and preserve.

And in addition to those written histories here in my State of Oregon, Portland State University's Library has, over the past five years, acquired a magnificent and growing collection of the private papers of a number of my state's women political leaders: Oregon's first female Supreme Court Justice; our first woman Speaker of the House; Oregon's first woman Governor; mayors, legislators, statewide elected women—*all* now in the collection of the library. This library collection will become an important research source on the political leadership of *one state's* women political leaders.

Again, like the Oregon Trail diaries, these personal papers will bring these women's lives out of the shadows: names, dates, photos, stories, history. So, with increased writings, autobiographies, extensive personal papers, what will we learn about our early women political leaders? Fifty years from now, when we ask the question again, "What takes a little girl from dolls and tea sets to the office of governor," will we have *more* answers, *more* stories, *more* knowledge? I believe that will be the positive result.

We will have the amazing story of Connecticut's Governor Ella Grasso, the only child of Italian immigrants and also a child of the 1930s Depression in her new country. We will read the difficult story of Washington State's Governor Dixie Lee Ray, raised with her four sisters in a household where her strict father constantly lamented having no sons.

Vermont's Governor Madeleine Kunin, born in Switzerland, left Europe with her widowed mother on one of the *last boats* transporting Jewish families to America. She began school in our country not knowing a word of English.

Each of our women governors has stories that are surprising, unexpected, clearly proving that they were not born to be governor, they were not anointed. And my story is no exception. I began my political career as a citizen advocate, a parent, seeking educational rights for my autistic son. My son had been sent home from school in the first grade—*not* for the day—but *forever.* His handicap meant he had *no right* to a public-school education and I could not appeal—not to the school board, the courthouse, or the state house. The 1960s laws gave my son no recognition, no rights, no recourse.

But I simply could not accept the unfairness, the inequity, the fact that my son's disability would be *exacerbated* by his also being uneducated. I spoke out publicly about this injustice. I pleaded for help. I sought a *hero.* I waited for a leader to step forward to champion our children's cause. By the end of the 1960s, I was a divorced mother with two sons, no child support, and a low-paying office job. But I was unwilling any longer to let those liabilities "short-change" my son. And I finally came to recognize, I had two crucial assets: a cause and a *mother's anger!*

So, I took a day a week off work (and the painful related pay cut), traveled to my state capitol and began a *fight* for my son's educational rights. I was politically inexperienced, scared to death. I didn't have the money to buy even a cup of coffee for a state legislator, but I marched up the capitol steps *determined* to change the world for these unserved children of my state.

I carried my message to every state senator and every representative. I pleaded for my son's future. And finally, my son personally testified at a legislative hearing. Mike told the senators that "special education" wasn't special for him. For him, *it was all there was!*

Five months later, the bill had passed both houses and had been signed by Governor Tom McCall. Oregon had the first such special educational rights law in the United States of America. That first political success for my son, *cemented* my belief that if your cause is just and you are determined enough and if you can make your case well—*one person* can make a difference in the political process. I learned it then and I believe it still.

As a young, poor, divorced, politically unsophisticated woman, I had spoken out and changed the lives of Oregon's learning-disabled children and their families. Plus, that experience as a citizen advocate had also changed *my* life.

Twenty years later, I was Oregon's Governor. An *unlikely* life story, but history is like that. I feel so privileged and gratified that I have lived in an amazing period of women's history in America. I have been both witness and participant. I have made a little history and now I have shared that history with my book, *Up the Capitol Steps.*

I will continue to share not just my story but the history, the remarkable stories of so many women who have changed our state's and our nation's history: pioneers, founders, marchers, suffragists, early elected women, women of color, women in Congress, on court benches, in governors' offices, running for vice president and president of the United States.

That history will not be left on a shelf, gathering dust. We must advocate for saving and sharing those inspiring stories. I fully intend to do my part, and I will in the years ahead. What I hope is that some of you will join me on this trail. And you could use as your inspiration, what I use for mine: I am inspired, always, by remembering the visionary motto of my state: "She flies with her own wings."

Certificate for descendants of the Oregon Trail pioneers issued during the Sesquicentennial (150th) anniversary of this historic trail, 1843—1993. Governor Roberts was awarded the Number 2 certificate, honoring her great-great-grandparents' journey along the Oregon Trail.

Speech Five
LOOKING BACK, MOVING FORWARD
NARAL Pro-Choice Oregon — February 2015

Introduction: I wrote this short speech as an invited article for the March 2015 issue of the *Portland Monthly* magazine. That issue focused on women and I was asked to submit a 700-word feature about women.

Shortly before the March release, I received permission to share the yet unpublished article with a women's gathering being held by the National Abortion Rights Action League (NARAL) Pro-Choice Oregon. The Saturday afternoon gathering of forty to fifty women was billed as a policy discussion that would include a "surprise unnamed speaker."

The invitation seemed casual and my being "unnamed" seemed to lower expectations for my delivery. It seemed to be a perfect place for me to read aloud my just completed magazine article. I had fun writing it and felt it would be even more fun to deliver to a progressive group of pro-choice women. And it was indeed!

In 2012, Oregon celebrated the 100th anniversary of our state's women securing the right to vote. Today in 2015, we can legitimately celebrate Oregon's women who have successfully gained leadership across a broad spectrum of arenas.

Yet, it is my belief that in order for these successes to continue to expand, we must acquire the historical knowledge

Barbara Roberts speaking at a NARAL conference.

of the women who blazed the trails on which we now tread. The deeper our understanding of those women, their voices, and their actions, the better prepared we will be to become "history makers" in *our* time.

Oregon history offers countless lessons that remain timely and profound in understanding the challenges and successes of Oregon women from all walks of life. I am reminded of:

- The hardships of so many Native American women;
- The endurance of the pioneer women of the Oregon Trail;
- The persistence of Oregon's woman suffragists who fought for more than forty years and five ballot losses to finally win the Oregon vote for women in 1912;
- The bravery of the women who fought for family planning rights;
- The strength of women who kept farms alive and built ships at home while their men fought abroad in World War II;
- The tenacity of women who challenged and won their right to a place in our law schools, our medical schools, our legislature;
- The scar tissue earned by Oregon women who held the first judicial positions, the first statewide offices, the first seats in our congressional delegation.

Hardship. Endurance. Persistence. Bravery. Strength. Tenacity. Scar tissue. *This is our history.* These women are our role models; they should be our standard for women's leadership today.

For let there be no mistake about the hurdles women in this nation *still* face. Here we are in year 2015 and the battle persists for "equal pay for equal work." Could any issue be more clear, more logical, more fair?

And forty-two years after the Supreme Court's decision on *Roe v. Wade*, we watch state after state in our nation add demeaning restrictions and roadblocks to safe medical access for this most personal of decisions for women. At the same time, television ads for Viagra and Cialis are all about beautiful people and personal timing *for men*. The equivalent personal timing and *safe* choices for women are clearly in danger across our country.

And when the 2014 federal election results finally crossed the "100 Women in Congress" threshold, the excitement was quickly followed by a major magazine cover photo and headline asking, "104 Women in Congress. Does it Matter?"

You think? Women are less than 20% of Congress. Would the women who fought for decades to gain women's suffrage think that the 100-women threshold was worth the battles?

How would our long-ago role models evaluate not just our gains, but our "slippage" in our unending battles for equal pay, for congressional seats, for child care for working mothers?

Historians could easily cite the voices of our foremothers as inspiration as we face the ongoing challenges for women's equity and our place at the table. Here are four illuminating women's quotations:

- **Suffragist Susan B. Anthony** made clear that our voices, our words, must be strong and determined. She declared, "Never Another Season of Silence."

- **Oregon Supreme Court Justice Betty Roberts** demonstrated the multi-generational legacy of women's rights work with her words, "I'm not passing on my torch. Get your own damn torch."

- **Amelia Earhart** reminded us of the huge importance of staying committed when she declared, "In soloing —as in other activities—it is easier to start something than it is to finish it."

- **Eleanor Roosevelt** gave us the defining statement about women's equality: "No one can make you feel inferior without your consent."

These quotations should remind all of us that we have unfinished work. We must find our voices. We must again light our torches and make clear our agenda for women's equity.

Our hopes are not at all unreasonable. Equal pay for equal work; personal decision making about family planning; more balanced representation of men and women in Congress and in state legislative bodies; and childcare for working parents. And perhaps, one day, a *second* woman governor in Oregon; and after more than fifty-plus years, a *second* woman U.S. Senator from Oregon.

The words of our state motto can be our guide: "She Flies With Her Own Wings."

BARBARA ROBERTS FAMILY COLLECTION

Barbara Roberts and Governor Kate Brown at an annual dinner for "1000 Friends of Oregon" in 2017. Brown assumed the governorship in 2015 and was elected in a special gubernatorial election in 2016. Roberts and Brown are the first two female governors of Oregon.

Section Three

A VOICE FOR OREGON

Former Governor Barbara Roberts at the dedication of the Barbara Roberts Human Services Building, accompanied by former Governors Ted Kulongoski and Victor Atiyeh, March 22, 2006. A permanent display in the building's lobby chronicles Barbara Roberts's public service as a legislative advocate for children with disabilities.

Speech Six

NAMING CEREMONY FOR OREGON'S
HUMAN SERVICES BUILDING
Salem, Oregon — March 2006

Introduction: The mall that spreads for six blocks north of the state capitol building in Salem is referred to as the Capitol Mall. Buildings that house Oregon's major state government agencies line the streets of that mall: Justice, Veterans, State Lands, State Library, Archives, Revenue, Housing, and more.

In 2008, the Capitol Mall became the State Capitol State Park, famous for its cherry trees amidst expansive green lawns and a variety of hundreds of trees, shrubs and flowers. The Mall is also home to dozens of statues and monuments honoring Oregon's history, including a new Oregon World War II memorial with a 33-foot-tall obelisk. In this park setting amidst Oregon's seat of government, Oregonians stroll the grounds, picnicking on warm days, relaxing in this beautiful setting.

In 2005, the Oregon Legislature passed a bi-partisan bill to rename one of the buildings in Capitol Mall *Barbara Roberts Human Services Building* to honor my early public work as a legislative advocate for children with disabilities. This was also the first Oregon Capitol Mall building to be named for a former Oregon governor. A permanent display in the building's lobby chronicles my contributions to Oregon human services.

On March 22, 2006, I delivered the following brief remarks at the renaming ceremony, focusing on my unusual connections to the DHS building, dating back to my first efforts in advocacy. Oregon Governor Ted Kulongoski and former Governor Victor Atiyeh, along with other elected officials and former Department of Human Services directors, were also in attendance. Former legislative colleagues and my family were present at the naming ceremony to celebrate with me.

The State of Oregon—my native state and the state of my Oregon Trail ancestors—has honored me a number of times with their trust, their support, and their votes. Today, thanks to the Oregon legislature, I am being honored for my long-term belief in the value of human services and for a *life's commitment* to serving those in need of our help. Being honored in this *lasting* and notable way is truly humbling.

Former U.S. Senator, the late Hubert Humphrey, used to say, "The moral test of government is how it treats those at the *dawn* of life (the children), those in the *twilight* of life (the aged), and those suffering in the *shadows* of life (the ill and disabled)."

To have my name associated with a state agency that meets that difficult *moral test* every day of every year, is one of my life's great honors.

It has been over thirty-five years since I walked up the steps of our state capitol to begin the fight for my autistic son's right to a public education. A low-income, divorced mother without child support, I knew personal and economic challenges—but I believed in fairness, in equity, and would *soon* believe in the Oregon legislative process. That first political success for me, not only changed my life, but changed the lives of hundreds of Oregon's disabled children and their families. That first legislative victory taught me that *one* person could make a difference in the political process. I learned it *then,* I believe it *still.*

The area of human services would remain always my priority—for the disabled, for health care, for alcohol and drug services, for the elderly, the terminally ill, for adoption issues, on the challenging needs of the mentally ill and for abused children, and for AIDS victims.

Delivering these special services has never been easy and will always be costly. But when others turn away because the needs are too unpleasant or too painful, this agency and its workers and leaders step forward and face these needs every day of their professional life. We owe these professionals our appreciation and gratitude.

But as citizens, we can do more. We can make the work just a little easier. When we reach out in our political capacity, in our communities, and in our neighborhoods and carry a small part of the load for a variety of crucial needs, we can *ease* the load. The opportunities to donate, volunteer, and serve are all around us in every neighborhood in Oregon.

It is my hope that whenever people see my name on this building, that they will think of our shared capacity to help the neediest of our fellow Oregonians. If, in some way, I can help deliver this message, I will have helped *earn* this honor I have been given today.

Governor Barbara Roberts listening intently during a meeting in the Governor's Conference Room, 1993.

Speech Seven
WHY ARE THEY ANGRY?
CITIZENS & THEIR GOVERNMENT
Savannah, Georgia — June 1995

Introduction: Six months after I completed my four-year term as Governor of Oregon, I was invited to deliver a lecture in Savannah, Georgia to the spring meeting of the National Academy of Public Administration (NAPA). This is an independent, non-partisan, nonprofit organization that assists federal, state, and local governments in improving their performances. The unique source of NAPA's expertise is its membership, which includes current and former Cabinet officers, members of Congress, governors, mayors, legislators, diplomats, and public managers who have been elected as fellows to the Academy.

It was a great honor for me to be chosen as a NAPA Fellow. The Academy promotes discourse on emerging issues of governance and I believe I was selected as a Fellow because of my state and national leadership on the issues of government reinvention and redesign.

The late 1980s and the early 1990s were a period of huge conflict between American citizens and their governments at every level. There were many problems, among them a lack of government transparency, failed communication with our citizens, an unwillingness of government to make positive changes, and a citizenry uninformed and misinformed about the huge expectations that rested on the shoulders of most governments and government leaders.

The lecture I delivered to NAPA gave voice to the frustrations on all sides and the cultural changes impacting our people and their governments.

Across this country and across the entire political spectrum, the battle cry is clear. "Government is the enemy."

Citizens are angry, frustrated, and disillusioned. They do not trust government and they do not believe their political leaders. This negative attitude about government is much more than a swing to the right, and it is more complex than just a growing conservative mood in the country.

This anger represents an anti-government attitude of proportions that may threaten our democracy if the trend continues. It is about the hatred and extremism that bred the tragedy in Oklahoma City.

This anger is reflected in the wholesale upheaval seen in the 1994 elections, from the Potomac to the Pacific. It is demonstrated by constantly dropping voter registration numbers and diminishing voter turnout in every area of the nation. It is voiced on talk radio, encouraged by TV and radio personalities, and cemented with voter-initiated ballot measures and state constitutional amendments, from Massachusetts to Colorado to California.

Politicians poll about it. Newspaper and news magazines write about it. Campaign consultants profit from it. Academicians analyze it. Government "reinventors" take advantage of it!

But let me be clear, there is a profound difference between cutting-edge reinvention of government and over-the-edge revolution against government. To believe adamantly in results-oriented, service-focused, smarter, more effective government, is to be part of the solution to the public anger we are experiencing in America. We reformers are not, however, the answer to those who want government to disappear, or who have no willingness to think or invest long-term.

Government reinvention and redesign, customer service to our citizens, performance-based programs, working across government boundaries, less waste and more results—those are the positive steps toward workable, supportable government.

Short-sighted cuts, politically motivated elimination of necessary but unpopular functions, inequitable tax changes, catering to powerful lobbyists and special interests, turning our backs on vulnerable populations—these are not reinventions, they are *regressions* and they will backfire, causing greater frustration, higher costs, more distrust, and even greater public anger.

We cannot reinvent government in America until the majority quit pretending or believing that it can be done with political rhetoric rather than complex reality. It is time to replace the *sound bites* with *sound policy.*

Too many political leaders are feeding the anti-government sentiment by telling citizens what they *want to hear* rather than what they *need to know.* Too many elected officials think all roads must lead to re-election and if they must direct enhanced public anger toward their political adversaries to get the election job done...well, that is the price America must pay for a politician's continued seniority.

In the meantime, citizens are caught in the middle, trying to survive, wondering where the truth lies, and who and what to believe, while being bombarded with stories of government failures, unethical politicians, and dirty campaign tricks.

To some, it finally means believing nobody—painting all government and politicians with the same broad brush while not registering to vote, not voting, not listening to the political din until—or unless—it reaches scandal proportions.

Good government, even when it occurs, is seldom news. It all seems pretty awful to the citizens of this country. And on the outer edges of that frustration has developed the truly anti-government fanaticism and the less active, but somewhat sympathetic, "question your government" attitude. And I predict it will get worse before it gets better.

In 1984, as majority leader of the Oregon House of Representatives, I decided to run for secretary of state. In Oregon, the secretary of state is also the lieutenant governor and the state auditor, so I knew it would be a hotly contested race. Republicans had held the office for 110 years and they were not going to hand it over to any Democrat willingly.

It was also my first statewide race. I was born in Oregon. My family came west on the Oregon Trail. I had traveled all over the state. I had recruited legislative candidates throughout Oregon, but I had never been a statewide candidate. On that fifteen-month campaign, I listened to more opinions, answered more questions, corrected more misconceptions than ever before in my life. I learned about geographic attitudes, gender reactions, rural versus city conflicts, and native versus newcomer biases.

In 1988, I ran for re-election as secretary of state and "hit the road" again. As one might expect, campaign-wise 1988 was easier than 1984. Although as secretary of state I had traveled the state constantly, I now found when I was really focused again, people seemed more concerned, more anxious, and more questioning of government and of information I supplied or presented. There was an "edge" I had not felt in 1984.

By the time I ran my so-called "unwinnable" race for governor in 1990, I had little question that the electorate had reached a "prove it," "show me," "says who" plateau more evident than in my earlier statewide experiences. Small anti-government, anti-tax, anti-incumbency groups attended many candidate forums and events. Everyone seemed mad at the federal government, regardless of party or philosophy. There seemed to be more confusion about what the role of various levels of government were: Geographic, gender, age, racial, and party differences seemed more evident.

The controversy over the listing of the spotted owl as an endangered species and the timber industry's reaction, hit Oregon with full force in the middle of that campaign. *Polarization* was almost instant. And the fires were fanned by both industry propaganda and extreme environmental reactions. The Endangered Species Act and the federal government were painted both as the uncaring perpetrators of economic disaster and the "puppets" of industry harvest pressures. Government distrust was growing by the day. Ballot measure petitions on abortion, term limits, hunting, nuclear power, tax limitation, the death penalty, and local government control were circulating in every county where I campaigned.

I supported the Endangered Species Act, opposed the tax limits, held firmly to my position against term limits and the death penalty, and opposed the anti-choice abortion issue. And I won the governor's race.

But I understood the distinction between *winning an election* and *receiving a mandate!* I also understood that if something was not done soon to begin to restore my citizens' trust in their own government, Oregon and its future were at serious risk. I was also quite confident that the problem did not begin or end at the Oregon border. And in the five years since 1990, that observation has proven to be more than accurate. America is *mad as hell* and they are not going to take it anymore!

The questions are: What are we, the ones who care about it —and who care how it all comes out—going to do about it? What are the causes? Are there answers we can develop to restore the citizen/government partnership in our republic? How do we create new avenues of communication? Can trust be rebuilt? And how do we expose some of the rhetoric for exactly what it is—rhetoric!

Well, I make no claim to be a social scientist, a psychologist, or an expert on citizens' political responses, but I do think there are some pretty clear indicators of how American government ended up with its back to the wall.

First and foremost, the anger has economic roots. Americans do not have as much spendable income as they had a few years ago. In most households, two people need to work to be where we were only a few years back with one worker's income. We are pretty certain our kids are not going to be as well off as we were—and neither are our grandchildren. That's important—and scary! *Fear breeds anger.* Someone must be to blame.

Then there's all this computer stuff—the super highway, e-mail, Internet, modems, cyberspace, lap tops. Large segments of our population have no idea what all this is about. It is threatening, confusing, overwhelming, and it makes people feel inadequate, or left out, or even stupid—and angry. And they react! This new technology is *not* a tool to make life easier. It is, in their mind, a complex instrument designed to put Americans out of work. It is elitist and foreign and not about an "honest day's work!"

And then there is the whole matter of an international marketplace where U.S. workers are competing for jobs and business expansions with workers half way around the world. And your workplace is talking about stuff like "TQM" and your plant is no longer unionized. And the new Japanese company across town is hiring at the same time your American-owned mill is laying off.

You come home at night and turn on the TV to find an Asian American broadcaster delivering the local news and a woman sportscaster giving you the sports news. These discomforts with change are all added to our life at the same time that crime and drugs and gangs, and even AIDS seem to be closing in on our communities, our neighborhoods, and our families.

For most Americans, especially white Americans, life does not feel as good as it did ten or twenty years ago.

It gets easier and easier to be mad about welfare, about taxes, about your kids' school, about the costs of a baseball ticket, a movie, or a government-purchased hammer or ashtray.

And Americans have been given a lot of reasons to mistrust their government. Since the Watergate scandal, we have watched highly placed government leaders accused, indicted, and convicted of illegal and unethical actions while in the service of their country. No administration since Nixon's has been without such scandal. We have seen equivalent behavior by members of the U.S. House and Senate. Television stories bring the transgressions of mayors, governors, state legislators, and judges right into our living room. And they all look alike to a disillusioned public who, as I said before, paints them with the same broad brush.

It certainly was not difficult to observe where these highly publicized political failures were pushing the public. And instead of government officials and politicians responding to the challenge of restoring trust, they instead stepped up the level of regulations, became more insular to protect themselves from voter frustration, spoke with more caution and less openness, and began to have an "us-and-them" mentality about their own citizens. Plus, those citizens watched as legislative bodies and the courts reversed actions that they had taken at their polling place on issues ranging from daylight savings time to the death penalty.

While legislators and congressional members received top-of-the-line health care packages, more and more citizens faced bankruptcy when their health insurance coverage disappeared. Citizens began watching with new resentment as county road crews leaned on shovels, lobbyists leaned on governors, and congressional members leaned on golf clubs at fancy resorts. Television told the stories—on location and in living color. And still, government waited to respond.

And as public anger rose, government became *defensive* rather than *decisive*. Government missed the window of opportunity when citizens were still ready to listen, still willing to give them the benefit of the doubt. And now that window has slammed shut, and we must work ten times as hard to be seen as half as effective.

But the work finally began a few years ago with what John Howard described today as "voices in the wilderness." Local government and state government began to seek solutions, look at performance, cut program deadwood, and bring citizens into the problem solving.

Neighborhood associations advised city governments. City and county governments consolidated some services. Some states recognized that fiscal audits were essential but performance audits were equally valuable. Governors began efforts on welfare reform, education reform, and health care coverage for citizens. State and local governments formed partnerships with private sector business groups to create enhanced economic development. Nonprofit service providers accepted performance standards when accepting some states' dollars. Campaign finance reform hit the ballot through initiatives in some states and were enacted by legislative assemblies in other states. None of these were enough, but they were positive beginnings for governments who had arrived late to the party.

It was in this climate that I arrived at the governor's office in January 1991.

My election night victory celebration had been tempered by the passage of a highly restrictive tax measure that had huge implications on the state's general fund budget. There was a Republican takeover of the Oregon House after more than twenty years of Democratic control.

As I have often described my election night, "It was the shortest honeymoon in history. I didn't even get a kiss."

But I was determined that we could handle the first round of cuts, we could look at tax reform as an option for future fiscal choices, and we could step up the performance audits that I had brought to state government as secretary of state. Plus, the new Oregon Benchmark process that had begun at the end of my predecessor's term seemed a great opportunity to move to results-driven state government. I was not the *"inventor,"* but I could clearly be the *"implementor"* and the *"expander"* for this wonderful and creative concept. And I do not think anyone would argue that I did exactly that.

As Chair of the Progress Board that develops the benchmarks, I made an important first decision: I appointed my Republican opponent for governor to the board. And for four years we worked side-by-side to make the Oregon Benchmarks a working, strategic set of tools for results and for effective government.

We took the first set of benchmarks to the legislature in 1991 and appeared before eighteen separate committees before they were passed unanimously. It took some real education to get to that point. We had to help legislators understand that benchmarks measure *outcomes, not effort.* In government, we tended to measure our success based on efforts (dollars spent or programs initiated) rather than on results. Not so with our benchmarks. Now we measure literacy and SAT scores, not education spending. We measure crime and recidivism rates, not prison beds. We measure air and water quality, not regulatory efforts.

Another critical matter, a highly important feature of this effort, is that the Oregon Benchmarks measures progress for the entire state, not simply for state government programs. The benchmarks are as relevant to local governments, community organizations, nonprofits, and business as they are to state government.

As we soon discovered, by their very nature benchmarks inspire the collaborative initiatives necessary for true progress on complex issues. Benchmarks inspired collaborative efforts on matters as wide-ranging as watershed health, urban mobility, teen pregnancy reduction, early childhood immunization, and internationalizing Oregon's economy.

Benchmarking is a new way of thinking. It is results—and solution—oriented. It cannot survive in isolation. It requires citizen and community participation. It requires both motivated public employees and committed community volunteers.

The Oregon Benchmarks are about vision, commitment, priorities, and measuring to goals. In Oregon, we took what began as a strategic planning document and turned it into this new way of thinking. Our state was learning the true meaning of collaboration because we now knew we could not reach our Benchmarks without each other. We were all partners in our state's future.

But as I approached the preparation of my 1993 budget and faced further huge cuts resulting from that 1990 ballot measure, I realized that investments in our Benchmark priorities were at risk. I also knew that the state government bureaucracy was just beginning to grasp the Benchmark concepts. So, I decided if I really believed and was seriously committed to the link between the Oregon Benchmarks and my state's future, I had to put my money where my mouth was.

So, I announced that every state government agency budget must reflect a twenty percent cut, but that seven percent [7%]—millions of dollars—would be placed back into agency budgets that could show a direct link between a priority benchmark and an agency program. The results were remarkable.

Benchmark documents became dog-eared as agency managers and line workers searched for connections between their agency and the state Benchmarks. You have never seen such creativity! I expected to have the Agriculture Department come back with a link between crop harvests and teen pregnancy prevention. We succeeded strongly in accomplishing two things; agency recognition of the Benchmarks and a focused, prioritized budget.

By the way, there was one surprising side effect: lobby groups, advocacy organizations, business, and nonprofits learned about the Benchmarks first hand. In order to support agency programs that they wanted to survive the big cuts, they were forced to become familiar with the state Benchmarks. That was a bonus.

Today, Oregon's 13 Key Industries have benchmarking for their own industry groups. Two of Oregon's largest foundations distribute money using our benchmarks as guidelines. City, county, and regional governments are now benchmarking, too.

The benchmarks are not a miracle; they are not a complete solution. They are not the only answer. But Oregon has found it a remarkable, comprehensive tool to prioritizing, budgeting, private/public collaboration, focusing, and results-driven government.

I have never been involved in a government process so challenging, so exciting, so far reaching, and so difficult to explain. Difficult to explain to citizens in a thirty-second sound bite, difficult to promote to media who see this as *process* rather than *product*. Difficult to explain to those who do not want to measure toward gradual success, but rather want instant gratification or stars in their political crown. Benchmarks are impossible to explain or sell to anti-government folks ready to throw the baby out with the bathwater.

But government reinvention, particularly in today's political climate, is not about "easy," not about public "credit." It is not about political careers. Reinvention is about a strong, committed, methodical march to a redesigned, more effective, results-driven, customer-oriented government.

And it requires leaders in every sector who are not afraid to gather a little scar-tissue on this road less traveled. But make no mistake about it, the reinvention, redesign, and re-engineering of government has another critical facet that we have not begun to tackle. We must find a way to bring our citizens back into the fold of participatory democracy. We must stop making excuses for why we cannot do it: We must just do it!

We must find new tools, new avenues, new opportunities, and creative paths to reach our shareholders and stakeholders in this nation. If town hall meetings and speeches and advisory committees will not get the job done. If they are not inclusive enough or interesting enough, we must invent new tools to bring government and citizens back to a place of mutual respect.

This may be the greatest challenge America faces.

After the 1990 campaign where I sensed the growing anger and apathy among my state's citizens, I began to think about a way we could re-engage our citizens and begin to restore their confidence in the work we were doing. I had made the first budget cuts, passed more than 95% of my legislative agenda, launched a task force of private sector folks on a year-long look at state government operations, and announced a goal of cutting 4,000 positions from our state workforce.

But with big new cuts coming, there was a growing push to reform Oregon's entire tax system. I was more than willing to face the challenge, but I was equally certain that most Oregonians would assume tax reform translated into a tax increase. I also knew that undertaking such a complex issue, one that must eventually end up on the ballot for a citizen decision, required the early participation of a cross section of Oregon's citizenry in a process that would have *public validity.*

From this thinking was born the "Conversation with Oregon." Thousands of Oregonians were selected randomly from voter registration lists in every county in the state. Huge public meetings were held to explain what we were about to do and to garner volunteers to help us make it work. The press was skeptical. Their first question was, "What if no one comes to the large meetings?" When thousands came, they asked, "What if no one volunteers?" When hundreds of citizens stepped forward to volunteer, the press asked, "What if you have more volunteers than you can use?"

Well, the volunteers did their job and before I knew it, I was seated in a television studio at Oregon Public Broadcasting in Portland ready to begin a two-hour broadcast to more than twenty-five locations in the state on Oregon's interactive educational network. The citizens could see and hear me. I could hear them, and they could hear each other in all twenty-five locations.

This process was repeated twenty-six times in every part of Oregon. It was believed to be the first such experiment of this kind in America's history. I cannot describe to you how I felt while spending this kind of time and opportunity to discuss real choices with my citizens. They were really engaged in the process, the issues, the challenges, and the choices.

Next, we analyzed all we had heard, reported to Oregon-at-large, did a second set of public meetings, developed a tax reform proposal, found supporters, and called a special session of the legislature to have them refer this constitutional amendment to the ballot. The measure died in the special legislative session. (It passed the Senate, but failed in the House by two votes on a procedural motion.) After a year of hard work, creativity, outreach, and real product, the tax plan was dead.

So, was the "Conversation with Oregon" a failure? I don't believe so! A detailed University of Oregon report found the process valuable and successful. Oregon received several national awards for this visionary effort.

We must find new tools to reach our citizens, inform them, solicit their views, involve them in our decision-making, and have them share with us in seeing the complexity of today's issues and solutions.

Restoring citizens' faith in government is about honest, effective, collaborative, results-oriented government. It is also about honest, effective, collaborative, results-oriented *communication* with the citizens we serve.

We are all in this together. We sink or swim together. The time of *us and them* must disappear from our vocabulary and our thinking. The term *"united"* in United States should be the pledge of government and citizens in every corner of this country.

Government must clean its own cage and open the cage door to the full view of America. We must do the public's business in public, and our citizens must once again take seriously the role of citizenship. They must share the responsibility for how this democracy works. Partnerships require investments on the part of every player. *We must all reinvest.*

We must invest time in our community. We must invest effort to become informed voters. We must educate ourselves in the workings of our legislative bodies. We must recognize that Democracy is *not* a spectator sport.

Good government depends on active citizenship.

*Barbara Roberts at Portland State University
where she was a frequent guest lecturer for classes in leadership. She also
served for five years as Associate Director of Leadership at PSU's
Hatfield School of Government.*

Speech Eight

PORTLAND STATE UNIVERSITY COMMENCEMENT ADDRESS

Portland, Oregon — June 2007

Introduction: I gave this commencement address for Portland State University's 2007 Commencement Ceremony for more than 4,000 graduates, their families, and faculty members. Prior to my address, the President of Portland State University (PSU), Daniel O. Bernstine, introduced me as the former Governor of Oregon and then awarded me the degree of Doctor of Humane Letters. It was my third honorary doctorate degree.

⌐⎯⎯⎯⎯⎯⎯⎯⎯⎯>

THANK YOU SO MUCH for this great honor. I am both elated and humbled to be recognized by Portland State University. Many, many years ago, I took my very first college night school classes at the Portland State Extension Center.

Years later, I fell in love with and married one of Portland State's founding faculty members, Dr. Frank Roberts. From Vanport College [the beginnings of PSU] until his retirement, Frank taught thirty-seven years for this wonderful institution. Finally, after my time as governor and teaching at Harvard University, I came home to Oregon and to a position at the Hatfield School of Government at PSU. Today, I feel as if I have come full circle and am now truly part of the Portland State family.

I have delivered thousands of speeches in my public career: some of those "rah-rah" speeches that politicians do; addresses to local Rotary and Chamber of Commerce groups; economic development presentations being translated into Japanese, Korean, or German; eulogies; inaugural addresses; and convention oratory. I've spoken to high school classes and senior citizens' groups, women's rights organizations, and brand-new American citizens. But for me, the most challenging of all speeches is the commencement address. Think about it: perhaps half of the graduates sitting here today are here to please their families and they just want to get this whole thing over!

Some of you may be focused on a big party tonight, or a flight home tomorrow, or a very long-awaited and deserved vacation. Commencement addresses are notoriously boring and often very quickly forgotten. So, what can I say to you—over four thousand newly-minted graduates—that will be meaningful, useful, and perhaps, even a slight bit memorable?

Well, I have to start with this admission: I have a history of telling citizens what I believe they need to know rather than placating them with what they *want* to hear. Comments on issues like taxes, reproductive choice, environment vs. economy, and personal civil rights are not usually designed for winning popularity contests. However, such challenging subjects are often the testing ground for leadership, personal character, courage, and ethics. So, for a few minutes today, I'd like to focus on the issue of personal courage.

Now, don't misunderstand me, I am not referring to the kind of courage our troops in Iraq must demonstrate every day. I am not referring to running into a burning building or diving into a flooding river to rescue someone. I'm talking about the kind of personal courage it takes to speak out when you stand alone on an issue. I mean being strong enough to refuse to laugh at jokes that demean minorities, women, gays, and the disabled. I'm talking about admitting your mistakes and not trying to bury them. I am referring to setting the record straight when the truth is being stretched, distorted, or just plain ignored.

Well, in that vein, this nation was recently privileged to see an extraordinary example of insisting on accuracy and truth. Most of you will remember the national stories about Army Private Jessica Lynch. In 2003, her American military convoy was ambushed in Iraq and she was badly injured and captured. Eventually, she was rescued by U.S. troops and celebrated as a hero, but when Jessica Lynch testified before the U.S. House Committee on Oversight of Government Reform, she courageously set the record straight. She spoke openly and clearly to the committee, saying, "I am still confused as to why the military chose to lie and tried to make me a legend, when the real heroics of my fellow soldiers that day were, in fact, legendary."

Think how easy it would have been for Jessica Lynch to accept the attention, the glory, the national fame—but her personal integrity would not allow her to accept the label "hero"; it would not allow her to ignore the truth. Jessica Lynch has demonstrated her personal courage, not only as a solider and a prisoner of war, but as an American committed to truth. She has honored her country and honored the families of her three fellow comrades who lost their lives during that ambush—*PERSONAL COURAGE* in capital letters!

Sometimes, personal courage comes in the packaging of political courage—and believe me, when it does, we should all applaud it! In this category, I am reminded of two amazing examples by former United States Senators, one of each political party, both from Oregon.

Democratic Senator Wayne Morse cast a remarkably courageous vote in 1964, when he voted *against* the Gulf of Tonkin resolution: one of only two U.S. senators out of one hundred. Two out of one hundred to stand up against the vote that led America into the political and military quagmire of Viet Nam. How different American history would have been if a majority of the U.S. Senate had been willing to join Senator Morse in that courageous stand of personal principle: a stand that cost him his re-election.

Three decades later in 1995, Senator Mark Hatfield was the only Republican in the U.S. Senate to vote against the Balanced Budget Amendment. The pressure to bring him back into the Republican caucus fold was tremendous. They begged, they cajoled, they promised, they even threatened, but Senator Hatfield didn't budge. He thought the amendment was bad public policy and dangerous political rhetoric. He voted "No," and tipped the scales that defeated that amendment. He took the heat and he took the guff for his choice, but Senator Hatfield calmly stood by his vote of principle. He was a model of both personal and political courage.

Personal courage can arrive as a surprise to any one of us. Our own personal courage sometimes comes when we understand that our silence is too costly. My entrance into politics began as citizen advocate, a parent seeking education rights for my autistic son. My older son Mike had been sent home from school in the first grade—not for the day—but forever. His handicap meant he had no rights to a public-school education. The law at that time gave my son no recognition, no rights, no recourse. But I could no longer accept the unfairness, the inequity—the fact that my son's disability would be exacerbated by his also being uneducated. I spoke out publicly about this injustice; I pleaded for help. I sought an advocate to champion our children's cause.

By the end of the 1960s, I was a divorced mother with two sons, no child support, and a low-paying office job, but I was unwilling any longer to be silent and to let these challenges short-change my son. My son needed my strength and my leadership, and my courage! So, I took a day a week off work, traveled to our state capital, and began a fight for Mike's educational rights.

I was totally inexperienced in politics and absolutely scared to death, but I marched right up those Capitol steps determined to change the world for the disabled children of our state. Powerful lobbyists worked against me every step of the way. I fought back on the grounds of fairness and equity. I carried my message to every senator and every representative. I pleaded for my son's future. Five months later, our legislation passed both Houses and was signed by Governor Tom McCall. Oregon had the first special education rights law for children with emotional disabilities in the United States of America.

That first political success for my son cemented my belief that if your cause is just, and if you are determined enough— and sometimes if you can be brave enough—one person can make a difference. I learned it then, I believe it still. That experience led to my career in Oregon politics, where I tried always to remember the lessons I had learned about speaking out, about standing up, and about willingness to change the status quo for the good of others.

Truthfully, most of us look at ourselves and we don't sense much courage buried within. But perhaps your demonstration of personal courage is waiting to test you just around the next corner.

Sometimes that test is thrust upon you. When President John F. Kennedy was asked how he became a war hero, he answered, "It was involuntary. They sunk my boat."

Yet, it is more likely that your personal courage challenges will come in a less spontaneous test of bravery or ethics. Martin Luther King Jr. made reference on a number of occasions to those kinds of struggles. Reverend King said, "Many people fear nothing more terribly than to take a position which stands out sharply from the prevailing opinion. The tendency of most is to adopt a view that is so ambiguous that it will include everything, and so popular that it will include everybody." King added, "Even those who cherish lofty and noble ideas, many times hide them under a bushel basket for fear of being called different."

Reverend King went on to say, "The ultimate measure of a person is not where they stand in the moments of comfort and convenience, but where they stand at times of challenge and controversy."

In 1984, I voluntarily put myself to such a test of personal and political courage. I was being sworn in at the State Capitol Rotunda in Salem as Oregon's newly-elected Secretary of State, the first Democrat to hold that position in Oregon for 110 years. I chose to have the Portland Gay Men's Chorus sing at that ceremony. I made the choice for two reasons. Number one, they were the most outstanding chorus in the state; and number two, I hoped and I believed if I took a stand of principle and courage on my very first day in statewide office, I would never fear again to act with needed bravery as an elected official. Twenty-two years ago, that was a real tough choice, but for me it remains a personal milestone.

So today, I encourage you, I urge you, I *beg* you to be ready and willing to stand up and speak out and take a risk! Take a risk to create a community, a state, a nation, a world that is more humane, more safe, more open, more inclusive, and more honest. Don't be afraid to rock the boat a little! Don't fear to color outside the lines when necessary! Have the courage to stand alone and understand what it means to have history be your judge.

As I said in my inaugural address as governor, "Each generation has but one chance, *one chance* to be judged by future generations, and this is our time!"

This is your time. Make us proud! *Make us proud!*

Speech Nine

Finding a Place: The Trials & Triumphs of the Displaced

Salem, Oregon — January 2015

Introduction: Willamette University, a highly respected private university and law school in Salem, Oregon, set aside a week in January 2015 to recognize and honor Dr. Martin Luther King, Jr. and his legacy and the lessons of the Civil Rights era that are still relevant today. The theme for that year's celebration was "Life-interrupted: A Look at Displaced Communities."

The law school asked me to deliver one of that week's addresses to be presented to their law students and faculty, plus community members. The speaking invitation indicated that my long involvement and commitment to disability populations, the LGBTQ community, women's rights, and equity for minority citizens gave me a wide range of possibilities for my speech. Their suggested title was "Finding a Place: The Trials and Triumphs of the Displaced."

I had thirty minutes to meet that challenging assignment! The problem was not filling the time but rather limiting my experiences and strong passions to the time limitation. When I completed the speech, I was given a standing ovation.

Barbara Roberts speaking on behalf of farmworkers' housing,
Nuevo Amanacer *(New Dawn), in Woodburn, Oregon.*

LET ME BEGIN WITH a quotation from Dr. King. Though made in the 1960s, it could well have been verbalized if he had observed America in recent months.

"Direct action is not a substitute for work in the courts and the halls of government. Bringing about passage of a new law by a city council, state legislature, or the Congress, or pleading cases before the courts of the land, does not eliminate the necessity for bringing about mass demonstration of injustice in front of city hall. Indeed, *direct* action and *legal* action complement one another; when skillfully employed, each becomes more effective."

Tonight, as I share some thoughts about finding a place for the displaced, about commitment to equality, about justice and fairness, about open minds and open hearts, I hope you will understand my need to place some of those thoughts in the context of my personal history. My life's classrooms have taught me many lessons—some profound.

I was raised in a loving home filled with respect and laughter. My mother was a farmer's daughter from Montana. My father was a minister's son from Oregon. My sister and I were raised without male siblings, but my father never thought he was "shortchanged" because he had no sons. Dad actually thought girls were real people. Yet, growing up in a small Oregon town in the 1950s did not represent the larger world I would encounter. I later found that women were often not treated as equals, respect and laughter were not basics in every household, and the all-white small community where I grew up was not representative of the larger world.

I was a successful high school student in my small school: school newspaper editor, cheerleader, service club president, student body secretary, class salutatorian. But nobody ever suggested I go to college. Girls in the 1950s—especially small-town girls—married young, had babies, and disappeared into the kitchens of America. And nobody questioned those choices, not even those bright, active, capable young women—not even them.

Today, women activists use the saying, "You can't *be* what you can't *see.*" Well, I certainly had no women role models in my community: No women on the city council, no women business owners, no women doctors, lawyers, CPAs, not even a woman on the school board. And certainly, no Oregon women held statewide office in those years.

When I visited the Oregon State Capitol with my 8th grade class, only large portraits of male governors were displayed on the walls. In the Secretary of State's office, the long line of pictures going back to 1859 showed only men holding that office. Not a single woman's portrait or statue was evident in the entire capitol building or on the grounds.

"You can't be, what you can't see."

Well, one day I would break that mold—but not before I had fought for my insurance and credit rights as a divorced woman, marched for women to be admitted as members of the Portland City Club, fought unsuccessfully for passage of the federal Equal Rights Amendment [ERA], and demonstrated for a woman's right to control her body and her family planning choices. I joined NOW, the National Organization for Women, the Oregon Women's Political Caucus, and even lobbied in Atlanta for the ERA. In Atlanta, while wearing a large ERA button, I was *spat on* for the first time in my life. It would not be the *last time!*

Many decades later in 2012, I actively participated as Oregon celebrated 100 years of Oregon women having the right to vote. The battle for suffrage in Oregon lasted for forty years, after failing five times on the ballot. During our 2012 Oregon year of celebration, I now saw that fight for voting rights through the lens of a fifty-year feminist. How grateful I was to the women and men who waged that long-ago effort in our state.

Efforts for social change can be long, slow, and frustrating. Sometimes, the need for that change can be invisible to those not personally impacted. Other times, the inequity is quite evident, but prejudice and hatred and bigotry—even fear—stand firmly in the way of change.

As a young mother, I experienced what it meant to be impacted by one of those "invisible" social injustices. I had two sons, born when I was nineteen and twenty-one. My older son, Mike, was experiencing some developmental challenges by the time he reached school age. A few months into the first grade, he was sent home with a letter saying he could not return to school. The school had no place for him and there was no place to appeal that decision—not the school board, the courthouse, or the state house. Laws of the 1960s gave no protections and no rights to my son, not at the state or federal level. There was *no place* for Mike.

I understood my son's disability would be exacerbated by his also being uneducated. He went through more medical testing and was labeled "severely emotionally disturbed." Later, he had a new label— "autistic." At that time, the so-called "experts" recommend *permanent* institutionalization. My little boy was a *throwaway.* I said, "No. *No!*

I began to speak out about this invisible discrimination. I pleaded for help. I sought a hero. At this very same time in American history, Martin Luther King was leading the movement for African American equality. I cheered his work and applauded his bravery. And I continued my search for a leader to champion the cause of children with disabilities.

By the end of the 1960s, I was a divorced mother with two sons, no child support, and a low-paying office job, but I was unwilling any longer to let those liabilities short-change my older son. I had finally come to recognize that I had two crucial assets—a cause and a mother's anger! If I could not find the leader I sought, I would assume that position by self-appointment. I would fight publicly in the halls of Oregon's State Capitol for my son's educational future!

So, I took a day a week off work (and the painful related pay cut), traveled to Salem, and became what I would call today an *advocate* for social change; an *activist* for *equality.* Five months later, Senate Bill 699 was signed into law by Governor Tom McCall. It was the first such special educational rights law in the nation. It was a full five years before the federal law passed for special education rights for children in all fifty states.

I had moved the mountain of government. I had taken on the challenge of creating change, and against all odds, I had made it happen. I head learned that *one person* can make a difference in the political process.

My son's educational rights were now *the law*. His needs and our cause were no longer invisible. Yet over the next decades, my eyes would be opened to other areas of discrimination that were often hidden in the shadows of our culture: mental health issues, homeless populations, injustice in the courts and with incarcerated populations, elder abuse, domestic violence, and end-of-life choices. Unfairness, inequity, discrimination, and social unawareness—*so much to do!* Such a great need for leadership, for heroes!

Earlier, I spoke of the long, slow, frustrating efforts for social change, especially when inequality faces bigotry and hatred. Such a battle has been evidenced in the social, judicial, and legislative efforts to bring equity and fairness to the LGBTQ citizens of this country.

Obviously, this prejudice goes back not just decades but centuries. Yet, the turning point in more modern times would likely be defined by the uprising against police brutality and arrests of gay men in the Stonewall Tavern incident in New York City. "Enough is enough" was the message and it generated a national gay rights movement that has never again been silenced.

The movement has faced tragedy and pain, but it has continued its relentless push for equality. The killing of Harvey Milk in San Francisco, the brutal murder of Matthew Shepard in Wyoming—even in death their message can be heard: "Enough is enough."

I have been an advocate and oftentimes an activist for LGBTQ rights for forty years. As a political leader, my support has been vocal, public, and proud. I have delivered dozens of speeches in support of gay rights here in Oregon and across the nation—Boston, Chicago, Vermont, San Francisco,

Minneapolis, Washington D.C., Los Angeles, Tucson, Santa Fe, and Dallas, Texas.

I served for six years on the Human Rights Campaign national board in D.C. I am a lifetime honorary member of the Portland Gay Men's Chorus—with one slight stipulation; the honor remains as long as I don't sing aloud!

I ride every year in Portland's Gay Pride Parade. Now, you might ask, "*Why?* Why all the support and passion for the LGBTQ community?"

I am not a lesbian. I don't have a gay brother or a child who is a sexual minority. But for me to remain silent because I am not personally impacted is for me to *accept* hatred and discrimination, for me to *condone* bigotry and pain, for me to *excuse* indignity and inequality.

It is not a matter of political or personal courage for me. It is a matter of conscience. For me, it works this way: I am a straight ally in the Gay community. I am a white ally working with communities of color. I am an advocate for people with disabilities of all kinds, even though I am not facing disabilities. I am an advocate for peace who speaks out for our veterans.

I have always believed we do our best work, and we are our most successful, when we stand shoulder-to-shoulder in our work for equality, fairness, and decency.

So, let me finish my story about being a straight ally for my LGBTQ brothers and sisters. In 1984, I ran statewide for the first time, seeking the office of Oregon Secretary of State. After a very tough primary and general election, I won the office becoming the first Democratic Secretary of State in Oregon in 110 years.

When it came time to plan my swearing-in ceremony, I made a big decision: I asked the Portland Gay Men's Chorus to sing at that ceremony in the State Capitol Rotunda. That was thirty years ago. It was a national first! This was so politically controversial in 1984 that the Master of Ceremonies asked me if he could simply introduce them as the "Portland Men's Chorus," leaving out the word "Gay"! I told him definitely not.

Well, I wasn't politically suicidal nor was I trying to create a media buzz, but the choice mattered to me for two reasons. First of all, they were the best choral group in the state, but more importantly, I determined if I took a stand of conscience and courage on my very first day in state office, I would never be afraid to do so in the future.

I recognized then that the work that had first brought me to the Oregon Capitol was about fairness, about equity, about opportunity. Now, as a state elected leader, I understood I would have a voice, a podium where I could help not only my own son but the sons and daughters of an entire state.

Through my six years as Secretary of State and my four years as Oregon's first woman governor, I took advantage of that voice and that podium. During my term as governor, I appointed fifty-four judges to the bench, including Oregon's first two Latino judges, our state's first Chinese American judge, five openly gay and lesbian judges, and the *most* women ever appointed to the bench in Oregon. The face of Oregon's courtrooms began to change.

But imagine finding yourself as Oregon's brand-new governor and being expected to fill over 1,500 positions on boards and commissions. Oregon's remarkable tradition of citizen participation is reflected in the tremendous influence of those policy-making bodies. But rather than the customary 1,500 appointments, I began my term with 500 vacancies left *unfilled* at the end of the previous governor's term. So, over the next four years I searched for more than 2,000 Oregonians willing to serve on predominantly unpaid boards for four-year appointments.

I was committed to bringing true diversity to hundreds of boards, many of which had never had a woman or racial minority seated on them since they were created. We could do better. We *would* do better. We *did* do better. During my four-year term, over 800 women and over 300 people of color became active participants on Oregon's citizen policy boards and commissions.

Yet, clearly the job of governor is about a lot more than appointments, particularly if your aim is to improve the lives of citizens facing extra challenges. But to make my goals for citizens-in-need, I now faced a huge new challenge of my own as Oregon's new governor.

On the same night I was elected governor, the voters of Oregon barely passed the most restrictive tax measure in our state's history. As I developed my first state budget, the restrictive Ballot Measure 5 [property taxes] cuts, starting with six hundred million dollars and moving to three billion dollars over a three-budget period, would devastate so much I cared about and so many plans I had for a kinder, better educated, more inclusive Oregon. I would be forced to make budget cuts in basic school support, mental health programs, community colleges, AIDS services, alcohol treatment, farmworker housing support, higher education.

I had reached a huge hurdle and a discouraging life lesson. In the words of Dr. King, "Human progress is neither automatic nor inevitable. No social advance rolls in on the wheels of inevitability."

I knew then that my four-year term would be about financial sacrifice. This wasn't a popularity contest; it was a race for Oregon's future! I had the voice, I had the podium, *and* I had the passion. *This was my time.* This was my home, my state. I had no intention to let Measure 5, along with the new listing of the spotted owl as an endangered species, and the resulting timber crisis, define the entire fabric of this place and our people.

Several years later after I had left office, I read a book titled *Leadership Without Easy Answers* by Harvard Professor Ronald A. Heifetz. A single sentence in its text described perfectly my sense of that period of change and adjustment that confronted my state and me as a new governor:

> "Leadership is a razor's edge because one has to oversee a sustained period of social disequilibrium during which people confront the contradictions in their lives and their communities and adjust their values and behaviors to accommodate *new* realities."

I would experience that razor's edge for the next four years! Yet, as I said earlier, we do our best work when we stand shoulder to shoulder.

As I began my governorship, I had a large, dedicated pool of talent available to me everywhere I turned. I certainly felt supported as I faced a long line of hurdles stretching into the future. And as Professor Heifetz said, "We must all adjust to accommodate new realities."

I asked for change, for adjustments. I just hoped I could deliver those difficult messages to Oregonians without someone shooting—literally or figuratively—the "messenger."

Now, I make no pretense as a leader that this was easy. I have the scar tissue to prove it. For example, in March of 1992, for the first time in Oregon history, a recall petition was filed against a governor—*me!* Not once, not twice, but *three* times!

In the first recall, the organizers were mostly connected to the timber industry. As the efforts continued, the organizers were joined by leaders from Right to Life, and then the conservative anti-Gay Oregon Citizen Alliance joined. Three recall efforts, gaining fewer signatures each circulation period, never came close to making the ballot, but they were disruptive, time-consuming and distracting.

My reasons for sharing the challenges of being a governor—from budget cutting to advocating policy change to fighting recall efforts—is not to demonstrate how tough the job is. Rather, it is an example of the many roadblocks that can slow down social change. It shows how a well-intentioned leader with plans to create affordable housing, develop employment training, change corrections policy, open teen health clinics, and promote diversity, can be sidetracked by non-productive and negative intrusions.

And we should also understand that money—or lack of money—frequently plays a large role in tackling the problems and needs of displaced and underserved populations.

It is easy to be frustrated, angry, and discouraged when we have causes—*people's* causes. When the needs are great, time feels short, when people face discrimination and feel pain, how can we wait? What is the value of patience? Is half a loaf of any value?

Dr. Martin Luther King, Jr. reminded us of the value of patience: "We must accept finite disappointment, but we must never lose *infinite* hope."

Half a loaf? Even a slice at a time is valuable! We will all find our place—our place of equity, fairness, decency, opportunity, and hope. We *will* because we *must.*

We *will* because Dr. King teaches us that direct action and legal action complement one another.

We *will* because we have opened our eyes—and hopefully our hearts—to those who suffer in the shadows of our culture.

We *will* because single voices have become huge choruses that ring out for justice and equity. They will grow.

We *will* because we will march shoulder-to-shoulder, bring voices of all ages and colors to courtrooms, school board chambers, city halls, decision-making, and *the ballot box.*

Like the Native American tribes, we *will* become oral storytellers moving each new generation to pride and to action as they learn of those who toiled in the fields of equity.

We *will* record and write and read of the heroes and risk-takers and leaders of social change who gave us new paths to travel. Where they have blazed trails, we will lay concrete. The better we understand the history of our heroes and those risk-takers, the better will be our own chance to make history.

We live in a state that has been described as "a laboratory for change." Oregon is recognized for creating national "firsts"; the initiative petition process, the bottle bill, our statewide comprehensive land use law, vote by mail, our death with dignity laws, and so much more. So many positive, innovative, forward-thinking concepts that make our state a better place to live.

Yet, none of that innovation happened without opposition, without criticism, without conflict. The changes we must make to achieve equity and fairness are not different. There will be opposition. There will be conflict. But together we can prevail.

Some changes will make headlines, like the 2008 election of America's first African American president; like the most recent news that the U.S. Supreme Court will review the constitutionality of bans on same-sex marriage in Michigan, Kentucky, Ohio, and Tennessee. The Court ruling will likely impact another fourteen states where similar bans are currently enforced.

The press coverage of Oregon's Death with Dignity law showcased a brave young woman from California. She was faced with a terminal brain tumor and moved to Oregon to legally end her suffering and terminate her life. This story will likely push passage of a similar bill in the California legislature this year. Colorado will likely follow close behind. Press and media will begin to note the growing momentum of Death with Dignity laws in America.

Some changes that help the causes of equity, fairness, access, and rights will come more quietly, but to those touched and impacted by the changes, they will be just as momentous.

I would like to share with you, as I close my remarks, a story from my governor's service of which I am very proud. It did not make headlines, but it made, and is still making, a positive difference in the lives of hundreds of families.

The preamble to this story began during the very challenging 1991 legislative session, my first session as governor. One of my most important successes in that six months was passage of a $25 million package to create the first significant, targeted state program to provide affordable housing for Oregonians. When I raised affordable housing issues during the campaign as a critical matter, no one seemed to be listening. I had said clearly, "Almost no human need is more basic than shelter. No family who *lacks* it can even begin to meet its potential. No community that *neglects* it is viable."

And the 1991 legislature heard my message and passed components to one of the strongest housing agendas proposed by an Oregon governor in decades. But within just a few months, I inserted myself into the middle of a new housing challenge. The City of Woodburn owned eleven acres of land that was originally planned for senior citizen housing. The development fizzled and the city was left with the acreage, a $252,000 federal grant, and an unpaid loan. For several years, the state urged the city to use the land and the grant to benefit lower-income residents. Time passed, the land sat vacant, the grant was unused.

In 1991, the nonprofit Farmworker Housing Development Corporation [FHDC] stepped up with both a plan and money to build desperately needed housing on the site. The city refused to even hear the details of the plan. In a community surrounded with agricultural lands and workers planting, irrigating, harvesting, and working in the fields and canneries almost year-round, the mayor and city council had *no* interest or intention of supplying housing within the city limits for those workers and their families. Their place was *not* in *Woodburn*.

Letters of complaint were sent to the Department of Housing and to the press. Litigation and formal discrimination actions were filed. The conflict was heating up. At that point, I stepped in.

No one could argue that the housing was unneeded. There was no other viable plan or buyer for the eleven acres. The location was quite near the high school and two elementary schools—perfect for farmworker families.

FHDC had a detailed plan for fifty family units and a childcare center. I endorsed the plan and the site and I directed the Oregon Economic Development Department to offer Woodburn forgiveness for the outstanding loan on the land *if* the city would transfer the land to FHDC. To my surprise, the city immediately refused. As governor, I was losing patience and informed the city that all future state economic development funds for Woodburn would be frozen until this issue was resolved.

After several other political roadblocks from the city, they finally caved. It could have been such a positive action for the city, but instead turned into a mean-spirited, stubborn conflict with strong racial overtones.

In December 1992 when the groundbreaking ceremony took place, I stood with my shovel beside my state housing director

Rey Ramsey, an African American, and the Hispanic FHDC board members. Not a *single* member of the City of Woodburn responded to the invitation. We stood ready to turn the earth for a $2.8 million housing project—the first, fifty-apartment phase of the plan—that would become *Nuevo Amanecer,* "New Dawn."

Forty new units were added in 1999, a beautiful new education center in 2003, and most recently, a leadership center. I have stayed connected to New Dawn, its leadership, and its families. I have watched with emotion as the first young people who grew up in *Nuevo Amanecer* accepted scholarships to begin college.

In 2009, New Dawn's leadership said of my history: "She was present and instrumental at the birth of *Nuevo Amanecer* in 1992. She believed in us when few others did. She used her power to do the right thing for us. She kept us in her heart and urged others to do so as well. She is our *'Madrina,'* the godmother of New Dawn."

What an amazing honor!

Today, the City of Woodburn and its elected leaders are enthusiastic partners in New Dawn. They are part of every ceremony and celebration. This project did not apparently warrant news coverage in 1991 and 1992. There was no headline, but we created a *place,* a *home,* acceptance, and opportunity for thousands of agricultural workers and their families.

Working together, standing up and speaking out, we gave an answer to what Dr. King defined as "life's most persistent and urgent question. What are you doing for others?"

My answer: "I helped create a place."

So, let each of us do *what* we can, *when* we can, for as *long* as we can, to promote equity, to enhance opportunity, to demand freedom, and to build dignity.

As I have spoken this evening, you have no doubt noticed the bell and dove statuette placed before me on the lectern. This is "The Bell of Peace" presented to me by the Matthew Shepard Foundation and placed in my hands by Judy Shepard, Matt's mother. The honor is called the "Making a Difference Award."

Imagine now, as I share with you the Bell of Peace, imagine Dr. King's words. [I then rang the bell and read the quote.] "From every mountainside, let freedom ring. From every village and every hamlet, from every state, and every city, *Let Freedom Ring.*"

[I rang the bell again as my closing.]

Barbara Roberts was awarded the Bell of Peace by the Matthew Shepard Foundation in 2010. The honor is called the "Making a Difference Award."

Barbara Roberts taught New Leadership of Oregon classes at
Portland State University, sponsored by the university's
Center for Women's Leadership. In 2018, this leadership class
joined Governor Roberts in front of the State Capitol in Salem.

Speech Ten

THE PRACTICE OF
LEADERSHIP AND CHANGE

Eugene, Oregon — March 2006

Introduction: This one-hour speech was delivered as a lecture to a class at the University of Oregon. It was one of a series of presentations affiliated with a class called "The Practice of Leadership and Change." There were thirty juniors and seniors in the class, and all were majoring in the University's Planning, Public Policy and Management program. The University also invited several student organizations to my presentation.

The professor said the class members were interested in leadership theory as well as personal leadership experience. The question-and-answer period focused on making tough decisions and finding unbiased information to aid in those decisions.

Students also wanted to hear my political "war stories" related to my leadership. I definitely had those stories to share.

TODAY, I PLAN TO SHARE some thoughts and views on the subject of leadership, talk a little about my own political career, and then I'd like to open it up for some "question-and-answer time." So, let me say first, that attempting to define leadership or to analyze leadership can prove to be an elusive process.

I've experienced over twenty-five years in public service. Plus, I've spent a decade teaching leadership skills and concepts to hundreds of state and local government officials at both Harvard University's Kennedy School of Government and the Hatfield School at Portland State University. That said, let me begin with my personal "shorthand" definition of leadership. It goes like this:

Leadership means having the *self-confidence* to believe you can make a difference, the *passion* to believe it matters, and the *courage* to risk it all, because you believe it matters.

Leaders should not be defined simply by their popularity, but by their willingness to take risks, their vision, their ability to share credit, their strength to admit errors or failures, their willingness to pick themselves up and keep leading and motivating and working for the broader good.

Leadership is not about quick fixes, clever slogans, dividing citizens, or about polling numbers. Leadership is about making change and about helping others *face* change. And to paraphrase Dr. Martin Luther King, "It won't always be easy. You won't always be surrounded by supporters when it is time to stand and lead."

And as many real leaders understand, you don't always receive full credit for your leadership, but that doesn't make the leading any less important. And finally, regardless of polling numbers, credit, or scar-tissue, real leaders step up and take their shots every day, perhaps understanding what hockey player and philosopher Wayne Gretzky once said, "You miss 100% of the shots you don't take."

Results come from *action*. Action is always a risk, but no shots, no results.

I have known many elected officials and many public leaders. I have observed them in times of success and in times of failure. I've seen them in moments of strength and courage, and in acts of fanny-protecting weakness. And regardless of gender differences, party affiliation, personality variables, or life experiences, *real* leadership comes through in times of choosing principal over politics.

There is no genuine leadership without *risk-taking*. Leadership is about having the courage to stand alone when necessary and cast a vote, take a position, make a controversial decision, when you are *not* part of the crowd.

Let me give you a couple of examples: Oregon U.S. Senator, the late Wayne Morse, cast a courageous vote against the Gulf of Tonkin Resolution in 1964. There were two senators out of 100 being able to stand up against the resolution that led us into the political and military quagmire of Viet Nam. How different American history would have been if a majority of the U.S. Senate had been willing to join Senator Morse in that stand of principle. That leadership cost him his Senate re-election.

And think about just one of the positions of former Senator Mark Hatfield. He was the only Republican in the U.S. Senate to vote against the "balanced budget" amendment in 1995. The pressure to bring him back into the Republican caucus fold was tremendous. They begged, they cajoled, they promised, they threatened, even to the point of threats to take away his coveted chairmanship. But Senator Hatfield didn't budge. He thought the amendment was bad public policy and dangerous political rhetoric. His "no" vote tipped the scales and defeated the amendment. Senator Hatfield calmly stood by his vote of principle. Leadership placed before political rhetoric.

Those two U.S. Senators, one a Democrat, the other a Republican, demonstrated political and personal leadership at its best.

As you study leadership, learn to observe and examine leadership among your colleagues, in your workplace, your classroom, your community, even in social settings. The more you are aware of leadership, the more you will see it, read about it, even learn to *practice it yourself.*

All leadership does not come in public settings with lots of bells and whistles. Sometimes taking a personal stand—for instance against the death penalty or in favor of gay rights—can be your own personal demonstration of leadership.

But as you observe leadership and leaders, beware of the so-called "leader" who gains followers by intentionally dividing citizens. Watch out for the "leader" who gains popularity by finger-pointing without any solutions of his own. And watch out for political and community activists demanding instant solutions while avoiding hard answers about funding, about the future, and about long-term impacts.

Another reminder about leadership: Leadership becomes more noticeable— more dangerous—and more important in times of social and economic disruption, in times of change. Think about that when considering the Viet Nam war, the current war in Iraq, the civil rights movement in the South, the great Depression of the 1930s, the spotted owl/timber crisis in the Pacific Northwest.

The visibility when citizens look to their leaders for big answers is the most-risky time of all to lead. Citizens want you to fix everything, to kiss it and make it well! And they want that to happen without asking *them* to make any changes or to make *any* sacrifices at all.

In truth, that is not realistic. Leadership is about change. And it is most often about helping others *face* that change and gently but firmly moving them away from delay and denial. Let me give you two examples:

During the 1990 governor's race in Oregon, the Northern Spotted Owl was "listed" under the federal Endangered Species Act. It was as if the Northwest had been hit by a terrorist attack; not so much the instant damage in this case, but the instant hysteria.

I was running for governor and the press immediately wanted to know my reaction. I was clear: I *supported* the federal Endangered Species Act. Well, talk about the you-know-what hitting the fan! *Never* in the history of Oregon had a political leader been elected governor without the support of the timber industry—our state's largest industry.

This issue was the most instantly divisive and polarizing issue I'd ever witnessed in Oregon. I'd been involved with the controversies of sex education, gay rights, taxes, and abortion, but none of them held a candle to the *divisiveness* of this issue. There was literally no middle ground.

Well, when you raise your hand and take the oath of office as governor, you pledge to abide by *both* state and federal law. Not just some laws. Not just the ones that are easy to follow. *All the laws.*

Plus, all the research I'd done clearly showed Oregon had been *overharvesting* and *under* replanting for four or five decades. We were also exporting raw logs offshore, giving those processing jobs to workers in Asian countries, instead of Northwest workers. We were moving toward a bleak, long-term future for the timber industry—an *unsustainable* future. The Spotted Owl was simply an indicator species.

Because I adhered to the law, spoke honestly about developing biologically-sound, legally-defensible harvest levels and species protection plans, I became the "bad guy." The timber industry and the workers from timber communities assumed I didn't understand their industry or their crisis, and that I didn't care about them or their future. The exact opposite was true. I came from a small timber community. I had immediate family members in the logging business. I knew we weren't going to fix this crisis with demonstrations, name-calling, and bumper strips about "fried owls."

The law required a recovery plan and I had to face the reality and the controversy of that requirement. The long and short of it was, as Oregon's governor, I sued the Secretary of Interior Manuel Lujan for refusing to implement our recovery plan—and I won.

We had to have a recovery plan in place if we were ever going to get *out* of the courts and *into* the woods to do any level of harvesting. My leadership, my adherence to the law, and my determination to find a solution resulted in three separate recall petitions being filed against me over the next year to remove me from office. The three recall attempts failed to get enough signatures to arrive at the ballot and the spotted owl recovery plan eventually gained the support and legal requirements to begin a new forestry practices harvest plan for the Northwest.

Under the Clinton administration, we secured millions of dollars of support for job retraining, economic revitalization for timber communities, and for developing sustainable forest practices.

It was the toughest policy issue I ever faced and I have the scar tissue to prove it. When looking for solutions to very tough policy issues, leaders must be willing to "color outside the lines." And when the policy issues are difficult enough and the long-term consequences important enough, a leader must not only color outside the lines, they must often color in *someone else's* coloring book.

Leadership is not a popularity contest. I promised you a second example about leading in times of change and about the greater risk when citizens are demanding instant answers.

We have such a situation currently confronting leaders and citizens in Oregon. You know it well. You've heard the demands for answers and quick fixes. You've heard the laments about the *lack of leadership* on this major issue. I refer to Oregon's funding crisis for education and critical public services.

Citizens everywhere in Oregon are appalled at the funding level for our public schools. Higher education tuitions are *up*. Higher education salaries are *down*. We have half the state police officers we had ten years ago. We are cutting the Oregon Health Plan, mental health services, programs for the disabled, alcohol & drug programs, and environmental services. County and city governments are also cutting services. And citizens are pointing at leaders demanding answers; the governor, the legislature, their school board and county commissioners. Citizens want leaders to *fix this mess.*

Well, let me give you a brief history lesson on this subject. Let me take you back to November of 1990. Measure 5, a citizen initiative, was on the ballot. Every responsible Oregon political leader had taken a position *against* this anti-tax initiative. Newspapers editorialized, recommending a "No" vote on Measure 5. Both candidates for governor, Dave Frohnmayer and I, spoke out against it. But, by a very slim margin, the voters of Oregon *passed* the measure.

Voters ignored *every* former Oregon governor's advice to vote "No." They ignored the editorials and the analyses. They heard only that their property taxes would be lowered and local schools would be protected from cuts. Leaders like myself warned voters that those claims were *unsupported* in the language of the initiative petition on the ballot. Sixteen years later, we know clearly those claims were untrue then, and now.

And if that wasn't a big enough *slice* of the monies for schools, local government, and essential state services, the voters went right on and passed three "get tough on crime" measures that *exploded* right in the middle of the state budget. Now, we lock up more inmates at a younger and younger age, for longer and longer periods of time. We hold a national record in the area of state incarceration of both adults and juveniles.

Those voter choices have meant millions and millions of dollars for new prisons, for hundreds of new jail cells, plus paying millions of dollars every year for staff to operate these correction facilities. And every dollar spent for those expanded prison sentences has been money taken away from schools, mental health services, state police officers, nursing home inspections, higher education, and job training.

These last few legislative sessions have been disappointing, frustrating, and unproductive. But before we start shaking our fists and voting people out of office, we need to walk to our closest *mirror* and examine other potential culprits.

You cannot pass measures like 5 and 11, and then expect a mostly inexperienced legislature to scale the mountain you've built. And by the way, legislators are mostly inexperienced because Oregon voters passed term limits and expelled almost our entire crop of experienced legislators from the capitol building.

So, when we think about public courage and leadership it might be well to give some focus to the word "public." As Oregon's public, we've managed to dismantle a fairly balanced tax structure, unfund a public school system that was turning out one of the best educated workforces in America, more than double our prison population, cut our state police patrol almost in half, allowed highway maintenance to fall by the wayside, harmed our higher educational system, and put our state's bond rating at risk.

Courage is a two-way street. How can we ask more courage and leadership from those we elect than we are willing to demonstrate *ourselves?* And no matter what you hear on talk radio, Oregon is *not* "tax hell." Let me give you the real facts about our funding crisis in Oregon government.

If you could turn the clock back to 1989, the year *before* the Measure 5 tax restriction proposal was passed by Oregon voters, you would find these facts: Research showed that of the fifty states in our nation and the level of state and local taxes paid by their citizens, Oregon ranked number 25. We were smack-dab *in the middle* nationally.

By 2002, a dozen years after the passage of Measure 5, among the states of the nation, Oregon was in the *bottom ten* states in terms of state and local tax load. *We were number 43* nationally, right down there with Mississippi, Louisiana, and Alabama. Our placement was certainly nothing to brag about! And Oregon being called "tax hell" was a totally invented lie.

Do we have a funding crisis in Oregon? You bet we do. It can only be repaired when Oregonians are willing to vote for tax reform to put us back in the *middle* nationally. The governor cannot do it. The legislature cannot do it. The local school board can't fix the problem. They can all lead us to a solution and threaten their political future when they take that risk, but *only the voters,* in the end, can fix the crisis. The "fix" requires a constitutional change that only Oregon voters can approve at the ballot.

So, when you hear a candidate for public office in Oregon running on a platform of *"No New Taxes,"* you better believe they are a large part of the problem and not part of the solution. Those candidates are not leaders.

As you learn to analyze and evaluate leadership, another important thing to understand and remember is that *time* is often the real test of a leader. Some folks look like leaders, talk of leadership, profess to have visionary ideas, and yet, when evaluated a decade later you may find that the evidence of that leadership is seriously wanting. *History* is often the true judge of leadership.

Let me now share with you what I think of as the basic building blocks for real leaders. There are nine of them and you could label them as "Roberts Rules":

Ethics and honesty matter from the beginning to the end of your leadership path. Don't be tempted by shortcuts to success and "just-this-once" options.

Even visionaries must do the hard work. A dream is nothing without the details that make it a reality.

The term "risk-taker" is not synonymous with a *kamikaze!* If you are going out on a limb—and leaders must—ask yourself these two leadership survival questions: Who has the net? And who has the saw?

Don't expect more courage from your elected officials than you are willing to demonstrate yourself.

Ask yourself when an issue really matters to you and you believe strongly that it's right, long term, "If I take this risk, what's the worst that can happen?"

Leaders can't lead without followers. Your treatment and respect of those who make you look good, do your bidding, believe in you, show you loyalty, carry your water, are demonstrations of your *leadership character.*

Understand and appreciate history—your own, your community's, your state's. You'll do a better job of *making* history if you acknowledge those who blazed the trails on which you now tread.

Think and act long-term.

Leadership is not a popularity contest.

I have given you some useful rules for leadership. I've shared some stories of making difficult and controversial choices. So, now let me share a quote that goes way back to the 1500s when Italian artist Michelangelo Buonarroti spoke eloquently about where we set our standard for accomplishment as leaders. He said, "The greater danger for most of us lies not in setting our aim *too high* and falling short; but in setting our aim *too low* and achieving our mark."

In fact, on the path many of us take toward leadership we will hopefully find a need to *raise the bar* several times as we, and others, begin to recognize and acknowledge our growing leadership abilities and potential. That is as true today as it was in the 1500s.

Leadership means making the choices on your leadership path. There will be roadblocks and detours, and even long delays while you do repairs. But if you believe in yourself, keep raising the bar, learn from other leaders, take on new and broadening experiences, and take the required risks. You can, and will, become the leaders we so desperately need today in our state and our country.

Speech Eleven

CLIMBING THE MOUNTAINS
OF CHANGE

Portland, Oregon — October 2009

Introduction: Most often, when we tackle the subject of leadership we speak of vision, new ideas, creativity, and even courage. Too seldom do we broach the subject of "change" as essential to being a strong and successful leader. In October 2009, I gave a speech addressing this topic to the Occupational Therapy Association of Oregon.

It was the first year of the Obama presidency and the nation was focused on change with our charismatic, first African American president. This speech was an opportunity to explore the implications of change with a group of professionals who work every day with bringing change to patients and clients. This seemed like the perfect audience and the perfect national climate for the topic.

I AM ALWAYS HESITANT to approach the subject of change. We may applaud the political leader, the new school principal, even a new minister who promises to bring change, but what we are generally applauding are the changes that *others* will make. Those ovations will end quickly when we find some of that change is expected to come from *us!*

Former Governor Barbara Roberts at the ten-year celebration of the Oregon Trail Interpretive Center in Baker City, Oregon, May 2002.

At this particular time in American history, we feel the threats and discomfort of change coming at us from *all* directions; the economy, the job market, housing costs, food safety, health care reform, international competition, and political unrest. Change squeezes us from all sides. Suddenly, slogans like "Time for a change" and "The change will do us good," do not seem quite so appealing.

After I retired as Governor, I moved to Boston and was on the staff at Harvard's Kennedy School of Government for almost five years. During those years, I worked with two faculty members who were especially creative and intelligent. These two professors co-authored an amazing book on leadership entitled, *Leadership on the Line,* with the subtitle *Staying Alive Through the Dangers of Leading.* The authors, Ron Heifetz and Marty Linsky, spent several chapters confronting the *dangers* of leadership in times of change. I'd like to share a short paragraph from their book that reflects on the difficulties of accepting change. Ron and Marty wrote:

> "People frequently avoid painful changes in their lives if they can postpone them, place the burden on somebody else, or call someone to the rescue. The hope of leadership lies in the capacity to deliver the news of pending change, raise the difficult questions in a way that people can absorb, and prod them to accept the message rather than ignore it *or* kill the messenger."

The two faculty leaders point out accurately that for most people change feels like *loss.* People are not simply resisting *change,* they are trying to face what they perceive as *loss.* We like what we know—the familiar. Habits feel like stability. They are predictable. So, in both one's professional life and even your personal life, you face change. Adjustments, new rules, new relationships, new bosses, folks from "outside" tampering in your work world and proposing changes that feel threatening. These are too many intrusions.

It is pretty easy in times as challenging as these to find yourself somewhat frustrated, perhaps even resorting to some good old-fashioned whining! Well, I have a system for times of facing hurdles, for times when I find myself actually whining. It is my system for what I call the "perspective check." So, come back with me to a long-ago time and I will share a story of hurdles, tough change, and perspective.

My family came to Oregon on the Oregon Trail in 1853. My great-great grandparents, James and Almeda Boggs, both originally from Pennsylvania, left their temporary home in Iowa that spring with a wagonful of their worldly possessions, an ox team, three children ages ten, eight, and four, and yet unknown to them, a baby on the way.

They arrived in Oregon six months later in October 1853, to accept their donation land claim in Polk County. By the time they arrived, they had buried their eight-year-old daughter who died of yellow fever on the trail, and my Great-Great Grandmother Almeda was seven-months pregnant. The child she carried for every mile of that arduous journey was my Great-Grandmother Anna, the *first* generation of my family to be *born* in Oregon.

So often television and movies have depicted tales of the Oregon Trail with whole families riding in the covered wagon. In truth, they walked—not rode—for six months across plains, barren wasteland, and rugged terrain in the rain, the cold, and the blazing sun. They walked across this continent. And along the trail, they witnessed so much left behind; cast iron stoves too heavy to haul any longer, beds and trunks, books and dishes, paintings, and even baby cribs. And most painful of all, the *grave sites*—hundreds and hundreds of them. The Oregon Trail has been described as the *longest graveyard* in the history of man. Graves left behind, never to be visited again by heartbroken parents and grieving siblings and spouses.

Now, when I think *my* world seems too tough, when I find myself complaining and whining, my tool for perspective is remembering my great-great grandparents and the sacrifices they made so that the generations that followed in my family could be born and live in this place that the pioneers called "The Eden of the West."

Most of us don't have to look too far to find those examples that remind us what sacrifice looks like. It's not likely you'll have to go back as far as the Oregon Trail to remember that better times will come again. Sometimes, the trick is simply *perspective.* I know that I probably sound like Pollyanna, but my life history has convinced me that we are able to make much bigger differences than we might initially believe of ourselves.

I grew up in a small town, less than 2,000 people. I often describe to folks that growing up in small-town Oregon taught me that everyone had to carry their share of the load. That's the way things happen in small towns. If you want to have a parade, you build a float and then you ride on it. Those early lessons *stuck with me!* I just never felt useful again watching from the sidelines.

And nobody, once I left Sheridan and moved to the City of Portland, explained to me that living in the city was any different from my small town. I thought that when I saw needs in my new community, I should simply *step forward* and help fix whatever was broken. I thought that was the way the world worked. Perhaps it's a good thing that no one told me differently!

My parents and my small town had set the example for me. Plus, I like to think there may have been just a little "pioneer spirit" from the Oregon Trail still flowing in my veins. I knew from way back in the Eighth Grade, when I studied Oregon history, that those pioneers did way more than just survive that huge challenge of six months on the Trail.

Families and neighbors, working together, established farms out of the wilderness. They founded the first schools and churches, the first orphanages and libraries. They built mills, general stores, and railroads. They established newspapers and court systems.

With this perspective, it certainly makes our challenges and changes seem more manageable. Our challenges today are *not* insurmountable; they are simply tough.

Like most of you, there have been times in my life where it became necessary for me to step up to the plate even though the odds were against me and I didn't feel I had the tools or the resources to meet the challenge. Few stories in my life better exemplify such a time of challenge than the experience that first brought me into contact with the political arena. It all began with a personal crisis. I was young, powerless, and discouraged. I faced a problem that seemed far beyond my control.

My older son, Mike, was sent home from school in the First Grade—not for the day, but *forever.* Mike is autistic and back in the early 1960s his disability meant he had no right to a public-school education. I could not appeal the decision– not to the school board, the court house, or the state house. At that time, the law gave my son no recognition, no rights, no recourse.

I simply could not accept the unfairness, the inequity, the fact that my son's disability would be *exacerbated* by his also being uneducated. I spoke out publicly about the injustice. No one heard me. I pleaded for help. Still, no one stepped forward. I sought a hero and I waited for a champion to lead the way for the needs of children like my son.

By the late 1960s, I was a divorced mother with two sons, no child support, and a low-paying office job, but I was no longer willing to let these liabilities shortchange my son. I finally came to understand I had two crucial assets—a *cause* and a *mother's anger.* If I could not find the leader I sought, I would assume that position by self-appointment.

So, I took a day a week off work (and the painful related pay cut), traveled to our State Capital in Salem, and began to fight for my son's educational rights. I was politically inexperienced and scared to death. Yet, I marched up the Capitol steps determined to change the world for the disabled children of Oregon. Five months later, Oregon had the *first* law in the nation requiring public education for children like Mike.

I guess it shouldn't be too difficult to understand why I believe in making a difference, why I believe change is not necessarily our enemy, and why I believe in citizen involvement.

We can change government policy. We can change people's lives for the better. And truthfully, if you didn't believe in change, you wouldn't be practicing in the field of occupational therapy. Every time you, as a professional, enter a care center, a school building, a hospital, a veteran's facility, a hospice program, a post-surgical ward, a rehab center, you are actively demonstrating your belief in change.

You understand more than most people in our culture that change can be painful, it can be slow, it requires adjustments, re-thinking, attitude examination, and often, teamwork. While it is sometimes tempting to wish for "the good old days," most of us living in reality know we cannot turn back the clock. Perhaps one of the few *constants* in life is *change*.

In my life, I have faced many changes: My son's diagnosis as autistic, the difficult end of my first marriage, the disabling condition of my second husband, State Senator Frank Roberts, and then his death while I was Governor of Oregon. There were so many hard-to-face changes.

But in a much more positive vein, I was sometimes the *maker* of change.

Governor Barbara Roberts with her sons,
Mark (left) and Mike Sanders, at her inauguration as Governor.

In the early 1980s, I was the first woman Majority Leader in the Oregon House of Representatives. In 1984, I was elected as the first Oregon Democratic Secretary of State in 110 years. And in 1990, I became Oregon's first woman Governor and one of the first ten women governors in America. Trust me, *that* feels like change!

Sometimes, we simply face change. Sometimes, we accept or adapt to change. Occasionally, we are the change agents. So, if I might share another personal story relating to change—historical change, cultural change, changing roles—let me take you back once again to my small hometown in the late 1940s and the early 1950s.

As a young girl growing up in Sheridan, I had no important women role models to follow; no women mayors, county commissioners, or legislators, and no women ministers, school principals, business owners, or doctors. But I do remember earning a Girl Scout badge for women's history and learning about Helen Keller, Madam Curie, Clara Barton, Joan of Arc, Eleanor Roosevelt, Susan B. Anthony, and Amelia Earhart. Reading about those women gave girls of the 1940s and 1950s new ideas to dream about—change that could actually happen to girls!

How different it is today! I look at my granddaughters and think about what they see, even in the women in our family:

- One of my granddaughters has a mother who is a professional chef.

- Seven of my granddaughters have a mother who is a judge.

- One of my granddaughters has a mother who has held statewide elective office.

- **And *all* of them have a grandmother who has been Governor.**

I personally believe those have been good cultural changes, but as we know, differences of opinion come with every change.

What one person or one group *celebrates* as reform, others may see as damaging, as unwise, even as threatening. Some changes we advocate for and some changes come unexpectedly. Some changes come in spite of everything we do to try and stop the change.

A prime example of this is taking place currently in the massive national debate over health care reform. How can you bring information and reassurance to senior citizens who are carrying picket signs that read: "Keep the Federal Government Out of My Medicare." That kind of fear and misinformation makes a conversation about change, about improvements, about reform *almost* impossible.

And how did the positive plan to fund doctors' consulting appointments with older citizens who want to understand end-of-life choices get turned into irrational fear about so-called "death panels"? When change is perceived as loss, it breeds fear and even anger. The reaction is often more damaging than the actual change.

Indeed, this is a complicated, challenging, even somewhat confusing time. Information and misinformation confound us. Legislation at the federal or state level could mean dramatic changes. One can hardly bear to watch the national news anymore.

The other day, I found myself thinking back to when my grandparents and parents used to talk about life during the Great Depression. While they certainly spoke of the hard times and about doing without, I also remember them talking about creating community pot lucks, about dancing to an old piano in the church basement, about playing cards and checkers, and helping the kids build a dog house out of old boards from a long-ago barn. Yes, these were clearly simpler times, but they were also times of changing one's expectations to meet the reality of that day.

Maybe that's what this last fifty years *hasn't* taught us. Perhaps we've lost the ability or inclination to *adapt*. Maybe that could be the source of America's whining and crankiness. Our country's seen tough times and come back strong. *We will again.* Yet, for a while we must adapt. For a while, we must work on our own perspective. I am reminded of the inspiring words from *The Diary of Anne Frank:* "How wonderful it is that nobody need wait a single moment before starting to improve the world."

In closing, I want to share with you one more brief story. I am currently deep in the process of writing my autobiography. The working title of my book is, *Up the Capitol Steps.* Having already completed one book, I had no illusion that writing this new book would be simple, but I reasoned that an autobiography would certainly be less painful and emotional to write than my earlier book on death and grieving. It sounded like a breeze in comparison. After all, I was there for every day of my life. All I had to do was record that on paper.

Well, I am here to say that I underestimated both the writing chore and the emotional impact this manuscript would unveil! I wanted the book to be a personal account, not a fully-footnoted historical document. I hoped my "small-town girl makes good" story would be both fun and perhaps, inspirational for other women and girls with big dreams. I was already picturing Meryl Streep playing my role. Well—*cut to reality!*

Writing about my parents and my only sibling, all deceased, made me feel more orphaned than I've felt in years. Reliving my divorce, my older son's diagnosis as autistic, the death of two husbands—*all* very painful and depressing. Plus, I've discovered that trying to recreate even the highlights of a life that now spans seven decades, is a demanding and difficult chore. It is a big story from a small-town girl. It is about a very long journey from my 1853 Oregon Trail ancestors through election year 1990—five generations later—when their descendant became Governor.

My autobiography is part history, part memoir, part politics, and part fairy tale! That has been the story of my life. I have been privileged to experience over twenty years of political leadership. I have *faced* change and *created* change. For me, they have gone hand-in-hand. And believe me when I say, I have the scar tissue to prove it!

Speech Twelve

VOTING: INCLUSION, EXCLUSION, CONFUSION
WHERE DOES OREGON STAND?
Oregon Historical Society — August 2013

Introduction: The Oregon Historical Society presented a summer of exhibits and public programs that invited Oregon citizens to delve into the complex history of citizenship. The organizers invited what they called "a dozen regional thinkers" to deliver presentations to explore the history of our citizenship and to consider what its future might be. I was invited to present on the topic of voting. The Oregon Historical Society's printed program described my presentation as follows:

> Former Oregon Governor Barbara Roberts gives the audience a history lesson, complete with "the good, the bad & the ugly" in Oregon's past. As a former Secretary of State in charge of Oregon's Election Division, she has experienced the state's more recent record of opening access to more and more voters. However, as a descendent of Oregon Trail pioneers, she is also keenly aware of the exclusionary voting past Oregon locked into the state's original constitution. She weaves those contradictions together and then measures Oregon's current voting law practices against our nation's 49 remaining states.

In 1984, Barbara Roberts became the first Democrat to be elected Oregon's Secretary of State in 110 years.

OREGONIANS, so often feeling pride in our state and its progressive history, may be guilty of wearing blinders about the less-than-positive history that encompasses our civic record on voting rights and citizen inclusion. We, as Oregonians, look at a long record of creative laws, many of them national "firsts," and respond to that list with some amount of smugness: The first initiative petition law passed way back in 1902; the nation's first bottle bill; our pubic, citizen-owned beaches; our statewide comprehensive land use laws; and Oregon's first-in-the-nation Death with Dignity law. We have a right to feel proud of our creativity, innovation, and public policy leadership.

However, looking back at Oregon's history of constitutional provisions and voting laws, there are historical legal restrictions that cause most of us to shake our head in disappointment. Now, don't get me wrong, Oregon does not stand alone nationally in voting laws that have excluded residents using racial, gender, religious, educational, marital, and economic excuses. Exclusionary voting laws have *clearly* been part of Oregon's history and with the recent decision by the U.S. Supreme Court to basically "gut" the federal Voting Rights Act, we need to be on guard for any slippage or damage to Oregon's current voting system.

So, let me take you back all the way to pre-statehood in Oregon. In 1843, the Champoeg Territorial government adopted a measure prohibiting slavery. However, the provision required slaveholders to free their slaves with the added requirement that all Blacks must leave the Oregon Territory within three years. This measure set the tone for several Oregon Constitutional provisions when Oregon was granted statehood in 1859.

Oregon's brand new constitution withheld citizenship and voting rights for African Americans, Japanese Americans, Chinese Americans, mixed-race residents, Native Americans, and in the case of voting rights—women. When Oregon became a state on February 14, 1859, we became the *only* state admitted to the Union with an exclusion law written into the state's constitution.

Just over a decade later in 1870, the Fifteenth Amendment to the U.S. Constitution granted Black men the right to vote, superseding the Oregon constitutional clause.

I sometimes think about that original Oregon Constitution in 1859 and consider my great-great-grandmother who walked across the continent on the Oregon Trail. She buried a child beside the trail. She was pregnant every step of that six-month arduous trek. She then worked side-by-side with my great-great grandfather to carve a farm out of the wilderness, but Great-Great-Grandmother Almeda Barney Boggs had not earned her right to vote in her new state. She was female.

By the mid-1920s, the Ku Klux Klan was flourishing in Oregon. Its membership was estimated between 14,000 and 20,000. The Oregon State Legislature, dominated by members of the Klan, passed a number of restrictive laws against first generation Japanese. While Oregon was focused on *exclusion,* the U.S. Congress was moving toward *inclusion.* In 1924, an act of Congress made Native Americans U.S. citizens for the first time.

A change of heart and a change of attitude in 1927 caused Oregon voters to finally amend our state Constitution to remove restrictions that discriminated against Black and Chinese American voters. While the efforts to end voting discrimination along racial lines continued, Oregon women had been engaged in a huge political effort that began way back in 1870 and continued for over forty years. Finally, in 1912 on their sixth trip to the ballot box, the initiative for the women's vote passed in Oregon on a 52% margin. The men of Oregon had finally voted to recognize the citizenship of their state's women.

Then in 1959, Oregon *finally* ratified the 1870 Fifteenth Amendment to the U.S. Constitution, which provided that no government may prevent a citizen from voting based on that citizen's "race, color, or previous condition of servitude." After almost ninety years, one can say of our own state, "Better late than never!"

And still later—forty years later—in the year 2000, Oregon finally voted to remove all racist language from our state constitution. It took 141 years to complete the removal of institutional racism from Oregon's Constitution.

Yet, all one has to do is look around the nation to know there are other routes to create hurdles and roadblocks to full voting access. Sixty years ago, it was poll taxes. Literacy tests were also used to block thousands of legal citizens from voting. Lengthy residence requirements disenfranchised thousands more.

Today, television news cameras have documented voters waiting for four, six, ten, twelve hours to cast their vote. A planned shortage of voting machines has turned legitimate voters away. Unrealistic required identification is now a growing culprit. In several states, college-student ID photo cards are rejected, as are photo IDs from public assistance agencies. State legislative bodies in North Carolina, Texas, and many Southern states are passing any law they can think up to keep racial minorities, college students, and low-income citizens from using their legitimate voting franchise. The day following the U.S. Supreme Court's 2013 decision on the federal Voting Rights Act, conservative legislative assemblies across the country immediately introduced state legislation to interfere with citizens' voting access and registration. They had been waiting with "bated breath"!

Now, I certainly know from personal experience that the desire to win is a powerful motivator. Television ads, mailings, door-to-door efforts, and radio spots give candidates and issue campaigns the opportunity to make their case. However, regardless of the will to win, winning should not come at the expense of citizens' right to register and vote.

Elections are not a game! Manipulation of registration laws, misuse of voting equipment, intentional polling location confusion, and questionable counting of ballots should never happen. Voting deserves 100% transparency and honesty. America, in all its fifty states, has not yet met that standard.

So, how is Oregon doing by those standards? Let's take a look at our state today. We were the *first* state in the nation to have vote by mail. It started out as an experiment, a test. There were lots of questions: Would it increase turnout? Would

Oregon voters trust the system? Would it give voters more access in smaller local elections such as school boards, school levies, water boards, and community college elections? Was this a safe, secure way to vote?

When the Oregon Legislature passed this voting experiment in 1981, I was a freshman member of the Oregon House. I had reservations about the security of such a voting system. Would spouses unduly influence their mates with a ballot open on the kitchen table? Would churches and union halls do mass-voting meetings without the protection of the secret ballot?

Those concerns would prove to be invalid as Oregon Vote By Mail laws moved from using the system only in local and special elections, to our first use of Vote By Mail to elect an Oregon U.S. Senator in January 1996 when Ron Wyden won the seat vacated with the resignation of Bob Packwood. The turnout with Vote By Mail was 66%.

In truth, from the first Vote By Mail Oregon legislative action in 1981, the movement to full vote by mail in all elections had a somewhat bumpy path. The 1995 legislature approved a proposal to expand Vote By Mail to primary and general elections. Governor John Kitzhaber vetoed the bill. Then in 1997 with Kitzhaber prepared to sign the bill, the bill passed the Oregon House and the legislation died in an Oregon Senate Committee.

Finally, Oregon voters took the matter into their own hands, placing a Vote By Mail initiative on the Oregon ballot on November 3, 1998. Oregon voters passed the measure for *full* vote by mail by a vote of 757,000 to 334,000—a very strong citizen endorsement.

When I describe Oregon's voting system to residents of other states, I describe it this way: "Oregon doesn't go to the polls; we go to the post office."

In November 2004, Oregon voter registration exceeded two million voters. In that fall's presidential election, Oregon's vote-by-mail turnout was 86%. It has clearly been a success in Oregon.

The other progressive arm of Oregon's election system is our voter registration process. You may pick up a voter registration card in most banks, public buildings, county election offices, most schools and libraries. This has been the case in Oregon since 1975. You don't have to have your signature notarized. Oregon also now has a statewide voter registration list online. So duplicate registrations can easily be checked from county to county.

In order to vote, however, you must be registered twenty days before an election. That has not always been the case in our state. Oregon actually had a same-day registration law that allowed Oregonians to register to vote even on Election Day, and thousands of Oregonians did exactly that. For ten years, Oregon's Election Day registration law worked effectively and flawlessly. During those ten years not a single Oregon voter was prosecuted for election fraud.

So why would a state reject an open, inclusive, successful voter registration system? What would cause Oregon to disenfranchise thousands of their voters every election year?

The answer is short: Fear of the unknown.

The fear related to a religious order with an East Indian leader, a guru named Bhagwan Shree Rajneesh. The Rajneeshees, thought of as a cult by many Oregonians, arrived in our state with plans to move their world headquarters to a very rural part of Oregon, east of the Cascade Mountains on 64,000 acres of rangeland. They had notable financial resources and were recruiting new followers, and they began building a community—a new town filled with members of their religious order. They also began purchasing property in the little town of Antelope, twenty miles away by dirt road.

Many things about these new residents seemed strange to most Oregonians, particularly in this very rural area. Their religion, their flowing red garments, their turbans, their large medallions with a photo of the guru, all led to an uneasiness that turned to fear. Then fear turned to anger and rejection.

The Rajneeshees began moving to Antelope. They began registering to vote in 1984 and then the questions began. Were these new people all American citizens? Were they residents of Oregon? Could you transplant busloads of street people from downtown Portland to Antelope, register them to vote, and take over the government of a small town? And could *opponents* of the Rajneeshees move their RVs from other parts of the state, create an encampment in Antelope, register to vote, and then offset the votes of this new religious order?

In November of 1984 by a vote of 69 to 27, Rajneeshee followers won the mayor's race and three of the six city council seats in Antelope. However, the much greater impact was the results this controversy had on Oregon's voter registration laws. In that same November 1984 election, I won the race for Oregon Secretary of State. My name had been on the ballot during that same period of controversy. That campaign brought me face to face with the fear, the prejudice, the anger against these "strangers in our midst." Folks reasoned if Oregon couldn't stop the "outsiders" from participating and winning, our system must be flawed!

In the 1985 legislative session, Oregon rejected our successful election-day voter registration system and replaced it with a ten-day cutoff. During the legislative debates and discussions, elected officials discussed cutoffs from ten days all the way to a sixty-day deadline.

I finally supported a ten-day cutoff as the best of the choices before the committees. It made me sad, even angry, to see this religious and racial bias used as an excuse for turning our back on thousands of Oregon voters wanting to participate in our state's election decisions. But it was clear that without this ten-day cutoff, even worse alternatives were waiting in the wings.

Following the 1985 legislative action, an initiative petition was filed, qualified for the ballot, and passed by a healthy margin on the November 1986 ballot. It replaced our new ten-day cutoff with a twenty-day voter registration deadline that remains to this day in Oregon's Constitution.

In recent years, you see numbers like these in Oregon: For our 2012 general election, 16,000 Oregon eligible voters signed up after the twenty-day deadline. Unfortunately, many voters do not become aware that an election is approaching until close to

Election Day. A dozen other states—from Idaho to Wisconsin to Maine—have ensured accessibility by allowing eligible voters to register at the polls on Election Day. Oregon is falling behind in voter registration numbers and voter turnout.

Where we once led the nation as voting access leaders, we are now caught in the 1980s "sand trap" created by fear and prejudice. Our current registration situation is reminiscent of the early days of Oregon's statehood when bias and fear closed voting doors in the face of racial minorities, foreign-born, and women.

I look at one of our other Western states, Colorado, and see a strong commitment to inclusion for all eligible voters. In spite of the objections of Colorado's Secretary of State, legislators and county clerks worked together to pass a bill that is the most expansive voting access bill in the nation:

- It allows same day voter registration.

- It requires every voter to get a ballot in the mail.

- It creates voting centers to aid first-time voters, voters with disabilities, and voters who have questions about process.

These centers make voters welcome and encourage participation. The Governor of Colorado signed the bill with great public attention and enthusiasm. Clearly, not all states and all political leaders are standing in the way of voter participation.

Here in Oregon, two other tools aid voting. Thanks to the leadership of Secretary of State Kate Brown, Oregonians can now register to vote online. This electronic tool saves paper, saves time, saves on staffing, and helps prevent information errors.

Oregon is also a national leader in the publication of our Oregon Voters' Pamphlet. Voting dates, voter registration dates, ballot measures, pro & con arguments, candidate photos and materials, and general voting information are put in the hands of our citizens. This pamphlet may be coupled with your Vote-By-Mail ballot to give you information as you mark your ballot. Good turnout matters, but an *informed* turnout is an additional bonus for good government.

So, while we are feeling positive about Oregon's online voter registration, a great voters' pamphlet, and a full, vote-by-mail system, let me throw a little fly in the ointment!

In the recently adjourned 2013 legislative session, Secretary of State Kate Brown introduced a priority piece of legislation on expanding Oregon's Voter Registration system. This bill was well-thought-out, carefully drafted, took some of the election-season pressure off the system, gave options to potential voters, and included security elements to meet the newer federal ID provisions. As I read the details of the bill, as both a former Secretary of State and a former Governor, I applauded this innovation in the Oregon tradition. It should have whizzed through the legislative session: That's not what happened.

Kate Brown labeled House Bill 3521 "Voter Registration Modernization." For example, the Oregon Department of Motor Vehicles' forms request name, home address, and birthdate. That same information is needed for voter registration. Sharing that information between two state agencies is a positive efficiency. The Election Division would then process the data received from the agency and register eligible persons to vote. The citizen would be registered as unaffiliated with any political party and receive a notice from the Secretary of State explaining how to *opt out* of voter registration altogether, or if they chose, how to select a political party. Simple. Efficient. Cost effective. Accessible.

Under the legislation, the voter registration process would be spread out across twelve months of the calendar making registration less cumbersome in the county election offices and more predictable for budgets and staffing at the local level. Secure. Inclusive. Non-partisan.

HB 3521 could easily have included 300,000 new voters in Oregon. Those voters would have been residents of all thirty-six counties. There were provisions in the bill for recognizing confidential records for those citizens with domestic violence orders or other law enforcement purposes. Privacy. Statewide. Citizen Involvement.

HB 3521 had it all. It had everything we could ask for in modernizing Oregon's voter registration system and expanding voter participation. Well, almost everything. After passing the Oregon House, the bill failed in the State Senate by *one vote* in the last week of the session. The bill lacked the votes that should have been cast, across party lines, by all thirty state senators. The bill failed on a 15-15 vote. I shook my head in great disappointment.

The press and media were almost entirely focused on tax issues and Public Employees Retirement System cuts as the legislative session ground to a close. Where was the outcry for voter accessibility? Who was speaking for the thousands of voters who would unintentionally fail to register in time in for the 2014 election cycle?

My speech title for today is: "Voting. Inclusion. Exclusion. Confusion. Where Does Oregon Stand?" As Oregonians, I hope I've given you some historical perspective, some sense of pride, and some reasons to stay alert and concerned.

Nationally, our U.S. Supreme Court has dramatically, and negatively, impacted American elections with the devastating Citizens United decision and the more recent decision on the protections of the federal Voting Rights Act. The impact of those two decisions will be the tools used to change the level playing field for electoral politics across America.

We must be aware and alert to any attempts to harm Oregon's election laws. We must be prepared to support positive changes when they come before the legislature and if they come to the ballot.

Secretary of State Kate Brown has said she will re-introduce her voter registration bill in the next legislature. Perhaps the question for us as citizens is: Will we be there to help?

When we ask where Oregon stands, we *must* first ask, "Will we stand up for Oregon?"

[Note: The Voter Modernization bill was reintroduced in the 2015 Legislative Session and passed. It was signed into law by Oregon's new Governor Kate Brown.]

Section Four

A VOICE FOR LGBTQ RIGHTS

PREFACE

THE THREE SPEECHES in this section tell three very different stories in three different states, during three changed cultural periods. In the early years, advocating for LGBTQ citizens was done in an atmosphere of hatred, anger, bigotry, and even danger. Witnessing the discrimination and unfairness, the blatant ugliness, and the legal mistreatment, made my silence *impossible.* Many times during my political career, I have spoken out for equal rights for the LGBTQ community.

Today, I witness an America where same-sex marriage is a constitutional right. I see LGBTQ members serving openly in the military, in the entertainment industry, in the presidential administration, and in Congress. In 2021, we are a *changed* nation—changed for the better.

Speech Thirteen

THE THREAT TO LGBT RIGHTS
IN OREGON

Eugene, Oregon — August 25, 1992

Introduction: In my second summer as Oregon's governor, the Rotary Club in Eugene invited me to deliver remarks at their weekly luncheon. There is usually a great deal of flexibility on the subject matter with this type of invitation.

The Rotary's expectation was the likelihood of hearing their governor address recent budget cuts, economic updates, and the ongoing harsh impacts of the property tax ballot measure that Oregon voters had passed in 1990. However, I had a different message to deliver, a message I felt Oregon citizens needed to hear.

At the time I gave this speech, the primary initialism was LGBT, which has since expanded to LGBTQ, and as of 2021, LGBTQIA+ to be more inclusive and representative of the wide diversity in gender and sexual identification.

GOOD AFTERNOON ROTARIANS and thank you for this invitation!

Over the last year and a half, I've spent a great deal of time talking about the pending service and funding crisis that Oregon faces. You all know what I think of Measure 5 and its required budget cuts and the negative impacts on Oregon, but there is *another* ballot measure just as destructive to Oregon: The Oregon Citizens Alliance's [OCA] Ballot Measure 9, which denies basic civil rights to homosexuals. This measure got its first foothold right here in Lane County—*your* county.

When the citizens of Springfield passed their "mini-Measure 9" this spring, it caught people's attention, even across the nation. Here in Oregon, citizens had actually passed a measure that placed legal discrimination against some Oregonians into their city charter. Almost immediately, backers of the measure threatened to scour the bookshelves of Springfield's library in a modern-day witch-hunt.

Why? Because the new measure meant there could be no public support for books that portray homosexuality in a favorable light. Plus, the city of Springfield immediately lost its liability coverage for discrimination lawsuits over one million dollars. And now, applicants for the Springfield Human Rights Commission face a litmus test imposed by some city council members. Apparently, there cannot be any human rights supporters on the Human Rights Commission!

And on July 3, the Oregon Citizens Alliance, the people who brought you the Springfield measure, filed a new ballot measure that could place the same restrictions requiring such discrimination into our state Constitution.

I believe in the soul of Oregon—that part in all of us that is optimistic and generous, fair and compassionate. But this ballot measure portrays another kind of Oregonian. It brings out the *worst* in us, *not* the best in us.

For more than forty years, I have been an outspoken advocate for my fellow citizens who are part of the L.G.B.T. community. I have spoken out for equity, fairness, dignity, and rights for sexual minorities who are part of every community and every family. This is not my time to become silent on this human rights crisis.

I cannot describe the shock and shame I felt picking up the *New York Times* last week and seeing the front-page headline: "Oregon Measure Asks State to Repress Homosexuality." All across the nation, Americans were reading that frontpage headline and forming an impression of our state.

And what would their impression be when, like Springfield, the entire state of Oregon began to purge our libraries, dictate school curriculum, and strip personnel policies of basic protections? Ballot Measure 9 says that government and schools "shall assist in setting a standard for Oregon's youth that recognizes homosexuality, pedophilia, sadism, and masochism as abnormal, wrong, unnatural and perverse, and that these behaviors are to be discouraged and avoided."

In that one sentence, the OCA actually directs schools to teach sadism and pedophilia to children so they can then teach that those things are wrong. And those judgments would also apply to homosexuality. This measure makes your local school board or your state legislature the "morality squad" for your family and your community. Measure 9 is not benign; it is malignant.

But if this personal affront to Oregon's soul is not enough to move you to the ballot box, let me describe another impact— the impact on Oregon's economy.

The day after the Oregon Citizens Alliance announced their state initiative campaign, members of the state Economic and Development Office of Film & Television were meeting with a film producer about a remake of the children's book, *The Incredible Journey*.

The producer picked up the front page of *The Oregonian* and said if the OCA had its way, he wouldn't be able to do more films in Oregon. And both *The Hollywood Reporter* and *Variety*, the top entertainment trade papers in Hollywood, have already alerted their readership to Measure 9.

This fall, Gus Van Sant, one of the most sought-after directors in the country, begins filming in Portland and Bend. If Measure 9 passes, cities couldn't issue permits for his film, simply because Gus Van Sant is Gay. Money, lots of money, that would have been spent in Oregon will go to other states.

In short, Oregon's fast growing, healthy new film industry will dry up.

Next year in 1993, the Oregon Trail 150th Celebration, which is being marketed nationally, is estimated to bring three million visitors to Oregon. But don't count on three million visitors if Measure 9 passes. Millions of Americans will boycott Oregon as they did anti-ERA states in the 1970s and early 1980s.

The National Middle School Association has put its $2.2 million 1993 conference, planned for Portland, on hold, pending the outcome of our election. In addition, the Public Library Association and the American Association of School Libraries are considering Portland for their future conventions, but both have made it clear they will go elsewhere if Measure 9 passes.

Tourism and film are the newest and fastest growing segments of our economy, and Measure 9 would dramatically affect them adversely. It would also affect our ability to bring new businesses into our state.

What company executive would want to subject himself or his employees to the McCarthyism of Measure 9? How could we attract the best and the brightest to Oregon? What would the stories about Oregon look like a year after passage of Measure 9 when reported in the *New York Times? The Wall Street Journal? The Washington Post?*

And for those of you who doubt whether the impact will be that great, let me remind you of another Western state where bigotry caught national headlines. In 1987, Governor Evan Mecham of Arizona rescinded the state's holiday commemorating Martin Luther King, Jr. Then, three-and-a-half years later, the people of Arizona defeated a measure to reinstate the holiday. To date, Arizona has *lost* 166 conventions and almost $100 million in convention business, and a Super Bowl worth $200 million.

And that's just conventions. Imagine the tourists that didn't bother playing golf in Scottsdale or visiting the Painted Desert. Or the businesses that located in Nevada—or Oregon—instead of Arizona.

Already, Measure 9 is affecting business in our state. I want to share with you a letter from a doctor in Cincinnati, Ohio, who has canceled his order for a $100,000, custom-made motor home from a Beaverton company. He wrote:

"Although neither I, nor my wife, nor my parents or children are either gay, lesbian or bisexual, I could not feel comfortable in doing business in a state should this legalization of discrimination be supported by the electorate....I really feel sad for needing to write this letter both because I am not happy about the potential erosion of our basic liberties, and because you have been responsive to my needs....Perhaps, should our basic liberties be upheld by the citizens of Oregon, we can do business in the future when I purchase my next motor home."

Instead, the doctor purchased his motorhome in Florida.

As your governor, how can I remain silent on this impending threat to our state's economy, our reputation, our culture? I have spoken publicly on this issue before. I *must* do so again.

I have stacks of speech manuscripts in my home office, each one making clear my position on gay rights. A large portion of those speeches were delivered in cities across the country while I served on the national board of the Human Rights Campaign, our country's largest LGBTQ support organization.

In order to speak out on behalf of LGBTQ rights, I sometimes had to cross protest lines. I have been called vile names and, on a few occasions, I needed police protection. My voice was never silenced by the ugliness of the anti-gay rights noise; it made my voice stronger to speak out for equity.

Oregon voters must make certain that our state remains a strong part of that *better* nation.

Do not succumb to the false assumption that you can afford to sit idly by and allow Measure 9 to infect Oregon's quality of life. Make no mistake about it, Measure 9 is about hatred, about ugliness, about discrimination, and bigotry. It is about a diminished view of Oregon. It is about threatening our economic future. It is about giving constitutional license for one group of Oregonians to sit in judgment of another group of Oregonians—and it is wrong.

Every Oregonian has a choice to make on November 3. As governor of this great and decent state, I am asking each of you to work hard to defeat the malignancy of Ballot Measure 9.

*[**Note:** On November 3, 1992, a majority of Oregon voters voted "No" and **defeated** Measure 9: **Yes votes:** 638,527 and* ***No votes:*** *828,290.]*

Barbara Roberts was sworn in as Oregon Secretary of State on December 16, 1984. She invited the Portland Gay Men's Chorus to be a part of the ceremony at the State Capitol. She was sworn in by State Supreme Court Justice Berkley "Bud" Lent. Barbara Roberts was an early outspoken advocate of equity for the LGBTQ community.

Speech Fourteen

BRINGING IT HOME: GAY YOUTH, FAMILIES, AND THE LGBTQ MOVEMENT

Harvard University — April 1998

Introduction: During my tenure on staff at Harvard's Kennedy School of Government, I participated in a day-long forum on LGBTQ rights, at that time referred to as LGBT. The program was part of the 2nd Annual Harvard Queer Politics Conference. The theme of the program was "Bringing it Home: Gay Youth, Families, and the LGBT Movement."

I was privileged to make the opening remarks to an audience of 200 students, faculty, and community members. The day's program included speakers from Gay and Lesbian Alliance Against Defamation (GLAAD). Author Andy Tobias who wrote a widely acclaimed 1973 memoir about growing up gay in a straight world, *The Best Little Boy in the World Grows Up*, plus writing extensively about financial investments and politics. Also in attendance were members of the LGBTQ Bar Association of Massachusetts and event organizers from the Kennedy School Class of 1998.

It was an exciting day and one of the most prominent Gay Rights programs ever held on the Kennedy School campus.

Today, we are here to focus on a pledge, a promise that most of us learned as children—America's promise to her citizens for their right to "life, liberty, and the pursuit of happiness."

Lesbians and gay Americans seek nothing more than a guarantee of these basic American rights—rights every citizen expects and deserves, yet rights that are still legally denied to gays, lesbians, bisexuals, and transgendered citizens in almost every city and state in our nation. Your community asks no special privileges, seeks no special rights. You simply seek an equal opportunity to have a good job, a decent home, and a loving family. This is not an *extremist* agenda. This is a *human* agenda.

Parents have high hopes for their children. We wish for their success and happiness. We want our children—gay or straight—to be able to choose their life's work and their life partner without fear, isolation, or discrimination. That ought to be a hope that *every* parent in this country can expect for their child. But your gay child has no such legal protection. No *legal* protection in the workplace. No *marriage* protection in their home.

In America, we should be able to expect more *for* our citizens and expect much more *from* our political and legal systems. America's promise seems so clear: "Life, liberty, and the pursuit of happiness."

And don't believe the rhetoric that these changes "can't happen" because the support doesn't exist among Americans for this "agenda of equality"; 74% of voters *oppose* job discrimination against gay people—74%!

Voters do not want to make it illegal for lesbians and gays to adopt children; 55% would oppose such a law. And 63% of American voters would oppose a law making it illegal for gay and lesbian couples to jointly adopt children. In addition, 52% support providing health care benefits to a gay spouse, and 62% would provide inheritance rights to gay spouses.

The numbers are clear: Public opinion is certainly *not* driving the wave of anti-gay marriage legislation. Only 13% of Americans said that passing the so-called Defense of Marriage Act, DOMA, should be an important priority. DOMA is the *extremist* agenda. DOMA opposes same gender marriage.

So, maybe the excuse for this ongoing injustice, the reason for this legal discrimination, rests with politicians' belief that their political career is at risk if they vote for fairness and equality for gays and lesbians.

Well, let me tell you, it just isn't so.

When the mean-spirited, divisive, Defense of Marriage Act came to a vote in Congress, sixty-two courageous members of Congress voted against the measure. *All* sixty-two members were re-elected!

While the current myth is that elected officials risk grave political consequences for standing against anti-gay marriage legislation, the actual experience is quite different. Let me give you three quick examples:

In 1996, in Colorado's legislature, House Minority Leader Diana DeGette led the opposition to their state DOMA Bill. That same year, she was elected to the U.S. House of Representatives by a seventeen-percent point advantage.

In 1994, U.S. Representative Sam Gejdenson, a Democrat from Connecticut, was re-elected by one of the narrowest margins in history—*twenty-one votes*. Two years later in 1996, he voted "No" on DOMA and still won his 1996 re-election by 15,000 votes.

Freshman Congresswoman Lynn Rivers, a Democrat from Michigan, faced a well-financed and tough opponent in her 1996 re-election race. In his effort to defeat Rivers, her opponent sent out two, districtwide direct-mail pieces attacking Rivers for her vote against DOMA. Despite these ugly attacks, Congresswoman Rivers won with 57% of the vote.

These are important political messages from our citizens. They represent fairness and equal treatment. The voters are ready and willing to support politicians who stand up and do the right thing—even when it is controversial. Times are changing. Attitudes are changing. America is changing. Americans are *way ahead* of their elected officials.

As the *New York Times* editorialized, "Chances are that Americans will look back 30 years from now and wonder what all the fuss was about."

I hope that's true.

For if the government has a "compelling interest" in this whole debate, it should be to foster stable, long-term relationships—both gay and straight.

After all, it *isn't* the gay community that is creating the 50% divorce rate in this country. If conservatives in America really care about *family values* and truly want to defend marriage in this society, they better find a way to stabilize and preserve the existing marriages and families in this nation rather than standing in the way of gay and lesbian couples who simply ask to marry the partners they love, and give these partners the legal protections, rights and responsibilities afforded heterosexual spouses.

Wanting a good home, a stable family, a lasting marriage, is *not* about gender—it is about love, respect, and understanding; it is about patience and communication. *Every* partner in *every* relationship deserves that love and respect, and if they are ready, the legal recognition by our culture of that love and commitment.

Gay America's youth need to feel respected and understood, and safe in their schools, their homes, and their communities. They need support—not the hatred and harassment that drives far too many of our kids to suicide, alcohol, drugs, and the streets. Fear is not a family value. Violence is not an educational strategy. Ignorance and false stereotypes and "head in the sand" in our schools are not a framework to promote acceptance, diversity, and respect for every student. And the courage of more and more students to come out of the closet, form student groups, and just be *who* they are, is one of the best educational strategies possible.

Today, you'll have a chance to hear one such student from Utah. Her story and the impact of her bravery and openness is truly inspiring. Kelli is my idea of a *real* hero. And the support she received from her family is a model of love and real family values. Andy Tobias, who is on this afternoon's panel, has created a video about Kelli and about the history of gays and lesbians that should be shown in every school and viewed by every American. Open the closet and let in the light! Kelli's story and Andy's video do exactly that. This conference today does that. Your being here, participating and learning, opens the door even further.

As Susan B. Anthony said many years ago in the fight for women's rights: "Never another season of silence."

And that is my message to Americans in every state. And that is my message to political leaders in every jurisdiction in this country: We cannot be silent in the face of hatred. We cannot be accepting in the face of bigotry. We cannot be apathetic about inequality and legal discrimination.

Today, you will hear some of this community's most articulate and committed spokespersons and leaders. They have written, spoken, defended, and led in the name of equality and dignity. They are bringing the message home to American on your behalf.

In Congress, in the courts, legislative halls, school boards, and corporate board rooms these civil rights leaders are building a kinder and gentler America. I am privileged to be a foot soldier in this battle for equality, dignity, and real family values for my fellow citizens—for gays and lesbians whose agenda is simply the full and equal citizenship that should be the hallmark of a great nation.

I cast my vote for equality.

Barbara Roberts Speaking at the Harvey Milk Diversity Breakfast where she was awarded the Lifetime Leadership Award in 2013.

Speech Fifteen
HARVEY MILK FOUNDATION
San Diego, California — May 2013

Introduction: These remarks were delivered at the 5th Annual Harvey Milk Diversity Breakfast held at the Hilton San Diego Bayfront. More than 1,200 people attended the sold-out event where the Harvey Milk Foundation awarded me the Lifetime Leadership Award. By 2013, America was a changed nation, both socially and legally, in terms of rights and protections for LGBTQ citizens.

On June 26, 2015, two years after this speech, the U.S. Supreme Court would finally strike down all bans on same-sex marriage and legalize same-sex marriage nationwide.

I AM TRULY HONORED and touched by this Lifetime Leadership Award in the name of Harvey Milk. I will place it in my living room beside my Matthew Shepard "Making a Difference Award." Two gay men who lost their lives to violence and hatred; two gay men whose openness, bravery, and honesty, even after decades, have left them to stand as reminders and historical role models of the kinder, gentler, more accepting and diverse communities we work to create.

I have been an activist and advocate for LGBTQ rights and issues for over forty years. As a political leader, my support has *always* been vocal, public, and proud. I have used my vote, my voice, and my endorsements to promote fair-minded candidates for public office and to speak out against those who peddle discrimination and bigotry, on or off the ballot.

You might wonder, *Why all this support and passion for the LGBTQ community and causes?* The answer is simple: For me to remain silent is for me to accept hatred and injustice; for me to condone bigotry and pain; and for me to excuse indignity and violence. It is not a matter of political or personal courage. For me, it is a matter of conscience. As Susan B. Anthony said 100 years ago in the battle for women's right to vote: "Never another season of silence."

Every time someone bravely steps out of the closet, that silence is broken. Every time we defeat ballot measures or legislation that discriminates against gays and lesbians, there is a huge chorus that breaks that silence. Each time we elect an open LGBTQ candidate to office—as San Francisco did with Harvey Milk, and as we saw with U.S. Congressmembers Tammy Baldwin and Barney Frank; and with State Representative Tina Kotek, who serves as the current Speaker of the Oregon House, who took her oath of office with her partner, Amy, by her side—those public choices turn up the volume.

Barbara Roberts and her partner, Don Nelson, celebrate Portland, Oregon's newly named S.W. Harvey Milk Street in 2018.

When President Obama repealed "Don't Ask, Don't Tell," trumpets broke the silence. When same-sex couples marry in states across our nation, bells chime and are heard across the land. It is an unstoppable river of change!

Now, I don't mean to imply that our work is done in any state in this country—far from it. We must challenge policies that harm gay and lesbian parents on issues of custody and adoption. We must continue to move forward to end rules or laws that discriminate against gay and lesbian Americans on tax policies, insurance, and immigration. From Stonewall to Wall Street, we must stand clearly for economic and social equality.

I have been, and will continue to be, proud to work side-by-side with the LGBTQ community, and with your straight supporters and allies in what I describe as the last great civil rights battle in our country. I will never be just a spectator.

So, let me close with a story both political and personal. In 1984, I ran for office statewide for the first time, seeking the position of Oregon secretary of state. In Oregon, our secretary of state is also the lieutenant governor and the state auditor. I gave up my role as House majority leader to enter this race. After a very tough primary and general election, I won the office, becoming the first Democrat to be elected secretary of state in Oregon in 110 years!

As we planned my public swearing-in ceremony, I made a very big decision. I asked the Portland Gay Men's Chorus to sing at the ceremony in the State Capitol Rotunda. Talk about breaking the silence! This choice was so politically controversial in 1984 that the master of ceremonies asked me if he could simply introduce the group as the "Portland Men's Chorus," leaving out the word "Gay!" I told him *definitely* not.

Well, I wasn't politically suicidal, but this choice really mattered to me for two reasons: First of all, they were the *best* choral group in the state, but more importantly, I determined that if I took a stand of conscience and courage on my very first day in state office, I would *never* be afraid to do so again. After the chorus story appeared in every single daily and weekly newspaper in my state, some political pundits predicted I would never be elected statewide again.

Well, in 1988 I was re-elected secretary of state, winning every county in the state. Two years later, I was elected as Oregon's first woman governor.

I was your advocate then. I am your advocate now. And thank you for this remarkable honor.

Section Five

A VOICE FOR DEATH WITH DIGNITY

PREFACE

Since the late 1980s, I have been a believer in, and supporter of, the Death with Dignity Act, the Oregon law that allows terminally ill patients to legally end their life with compassion and dignity. My late husband, State Senator Frank Roberts, was a leading public proponent of this end-of-life choice and introduced legislation in the Oregon senate three times between 1987 and 1991.

Frank died of cancer in 1993 and I remained a supporter of his unfinished work. I endorsed the Oregon ballot measure as governor in 1994 when it was before the Oregon voters for their decision. The ballot measure passed! Three years later in 1997, Oregon voters rejected the state legislature's attempt to repeal the law with 60% of voters supporting the measure for a second time. Oregon's Death with Dignity law was a *national first.*

Since 1997, I have followed closely the application of Oregon's law and have remained a vocal advocate of this legal end-of-life choice. The first and second editions of my book *Death Without Denial, Grief Without Apology* shared some of the history of this law and how it has gained momentum and acceptance in other states as an end-of-life choice.

Oregon stood alone for several years as the *only* state with a Death with Dignity law. However, in recent years the nation's citizenry has evolved a growing awareness and a support of end-of-life choices. We are witnessing a new movement in America.

The strongest support for end-of-life laws began in the Western states. As of July 2021, Oregon, Washington, California, Hawaii, Montana, Colorado, and New Mexico have death with dignity statutes. Supportive Eastern states include Vermont, the District of Columbia, and New Jersey. And more than a dozen other states are currently considering death with dignity legislation. Oregon no longer stands alone on this compassionate issue.

Some of the many facets of Oregon's experience, and my advocacy in other parts of the nation, are shared in this section of the book. What follows are excerpts from speeches in five different states where I spoke in support of their state's caring and compassionate legal proposals.

Speech Sixteen

AMERICAN ACADEMY OF BEREAVEMENT CONFERENCE

Phoenix, Arizona — October 2005

GOOD MORNING, THANK YOU for your warm welcome, and for allowing me this podium before an audience for whom I have both respect and admiration.

Since my book on death and grieving was published three years ago, I've spoken to hundreds of audiences—hospice programs, AIDS groups, hospital staffs, college classrooms, book clubs, senior citizen organizations, even several business groups. And as you can well imagine, some of these audiences were quite uncomfortable in actually *facing* the subjects of death and grief, but clearly this audience is an exception to that reaction.

You do the work every day that I try to present in an open, personal, even comfortable way to audiences every chance I get. But I make no pretense about being an expert on this subject area. *You* are the experts, however, as an author of a book on the subject of death and grieving, I've listened to hundreds of end-of-life stories and the tales of the grief that followed.

Yet, if there is anything Americans wish to avoid discussing, find more threatening to face, and routinely skip making preparations for, it is our *own* inevitable death. However, having said that, I believe the United States is today a changing nation on the subject of death.

Governor Barbara Roberts with her husband State Senator Frank Roberts in the governor's office, 1992. Both of them supported Death with Dignity.

Over the past few years, our citizens have been bombarded with chilling scenes of death and loss right here at home. The bombing of the federal building in Oklahoma City and the moving photo we all remember of a grieving Oklahoma fireman carrying the small body of a lifeless toddler out of the devastation. That became an indelible memory for millions of Americans.

Television also gave us up-close coverage of school shootings across the nation. We watched as children screamed in fear and horror, and grieved openly over the bodies of their classmates. And then the shocking terrorists' attacks that *rocked* the United States on September 11, 2001, again reminded us of the tentative hold we each have on life.

We have, through television, attended the funerals and seen the public memorials for hundreds of those lost to those senseless brutalities. Yet, in reality the deaths most of us will experience in our lifetime, those of disease, illness, and old age, are markedly different from those deaths of violence we have seen on television.

However acknowledged, I still sense we are a nation more aware and more accepting, and with a more realistic grasp of the end of life. Death is no longer a total stranger!

Speech Seventeen
ASSOCIATION FOR DEATH EDUCATION & COUNSELING CONFERENCE

Albuquerque, New Mexico — April 2005

WHETHER PEOPLE SUPPORT OR OPPOSE Oregon's Death with Dignity law, no one can deny the impact it has had on end-of-life issues in my state. It is a shining example of my adage: *What we can talk about, we can indeed make better.*

Let me give you a sense of that period in Oregon in the 1990s when Oregonians were considering this issue. When Death with Dignity came to the Oregon ballot, there were two, heavily-financed statewide campaigns. *Very controversial!* There were constant debates, television and radio ads, newspaper articles, and speeches. It was the biggest issue happening in Oregon.

As a result of those two ballot campaigns, Oregon voters became the best-informed Americans in any of our fifty states on the subjects of dying, pain medication, heroic medical procedures, advance directives, and hospice care. Dying was discussed over dinner, in bowling alleys, at hair salons and barbershops, in gyms, classrooms, and churches.

Once families had opened those discussions, they couldn't put the toothpaste back in the tube. Lawyers were suddenly drafting more wills, more medical directives, and recording medical powers of attorney. Soon, highly informed patients were asking their physicians to explain their attitudes and positions on "do not resuscitate orders" and Oregon's new Death with Dignity law, plus the issue of pain management. As Oregon families and patients gained a greater understanding of medical matters and end-of-life choices, they now had greater expectations of their medical providers.

In 2004, the Oregon Health & Science University medical school's Center for Ethics in Health Care published a monograph entitled *The Oregon Report Card: Improving Care of the Dying*. The study interviewed over 500 Oregon families who had recently lost an adult family member to illness, disease, or old age. Researchers were attempting to identify barriers to improving care for the dying from the family's perspective. Let me just share a few things we learned from that study.

Families felt that medical providers in our state were doing an excellent job of encouraging advanced planning and then *honoring* the treatment wishes of the patient at the end of life. They felt physicians and hospitals were now more committed to giving patients the *exit* they wished to experience.

The report also showed Oregon's high use of hospice care and pain medication for dying patients—*both* the highest in the nation. Families felt these two facts had given their loved ones' calm, dignified, pain-free deaths.

However, there were two issues of concern in the report regarding hospice. Since hospice care requires a determination of less than six months to live, some patients and families were unwilling or reluctant to accept that prognosis. Loved ones may be unwilling to *give up* on aggressive treatments. As a result, many patients are living—and dying—in a state of denial.

Unfortunately, many physicians join with patients and families in avoiding a painful but real conversation about a terminal prognosis. Many physicians see death as a *defeat* and are reluctant to accept death as a normal part of life.

The Oregon study showed that this reluctance caused extended delays in a patient entering hospice care. That delay means not only extra unnecessary financial burdens on many families, but more importantly, the lack of in-home support that hospice provides for both patients and their family caregivers, plus the emotional support so important to prepare for the dying process. Hospice should be seen as a friend to both patient and physician. *Denial is not that friend.*

I tell doctors that hospice offers a quality medical *transition* and with that honest recommendation, they are handing their patients a *gift* of truth and support. In the highly emotional and trying period at end of life, someone has to be the adult. And who better to deliver those difficult messages than a trusted physician?

Terminal patients deserve honesty and openness. They deserve information and choices. They deserve respect; *both* medical providers and family members should deliver that respect.

And let me say this about choice: A large number of terminally ill Oregonians have gone through the required legal and medical procedures to obtain the medication under the Death with Dignity Law and then have chosen *not* to use the prescription to end their life. It became more and more clear that patients found *real comfort* in knowing they had the option. In the end, the decision was theirs.

From the beginning, self-determination was a vitally important element of the Oregon Death with Dignity law.

Speech Eighteen

PRESS CONFERENCE ON DEATH WITH DIGNITY

San Francisco, California — April 2006

As OREGON'S GOVERNOR from 1991 to 1995, I served at the time of the passage of Oregon's Death with Dignity law. Calling on that experience, I had the opportunity in April of last year to testify before the California Assembly's Judiciary Committee in support of California's proposed Compassionate Choices legislation.

I am here again today from your neighboring state of Oregon to add my support to Assembly Bill 651, your state's compassionate choices legislation. I am also here today to share my state's experience to date with our landmark Death with Dignity Act, plus some of the benefits that have come to Oregon and to our people.

Since the passage of Oregon's law, we have seen many positive changes in the arena of end-of-life issues. First of all, the use of hospice for terminally ill Oregonians increased notably. High-quality hospice care is now available in *every* county in our state. Today, Oregon has one of the highest-hospice uses in the country. More citizens in Oregon die at home than die in hospitals. For families and patients, this change has given dignity, comfort, and pain-free exits to so many of our citizens.

Also, since Oregon's law passed, our state's use of much-needed pain medication for terminal patients is one of the highest in the nation. It has become clear that Oregon's vastly improved pain management system has allowed more *quality* time for patients and their loved ones.

In terms of end-of-life matters, it is becoming obvious in Oregon that what we can talk about, we can make better. I believe strongly that the same will be said of California as your legislature debates and passes AB 651. Oregon's law has been upheld through every state and federal court challenge, including the most recent decision before the United States Supreme Court.

However, the court of public opinion has also been relevant with Oregon's law. Our citizenry, our political leaders, our medical community, and our disability community are *all* strongly supportive of Oregon's law. That support has constantly increased as Oregonians have witnessed the law being used sparingly and with adherence to both the *letter* and the *spirit* of our unique law.

To give you a sense of how Oregon's Death with Dignity law has worked over the first eight years, consider this: about 30,000 Oregonians die each year, and during those eight years, about 240,000 of our citizens died, however, only 246 terminally ill patients hastened their death with Oregon's law. *All* of those who died had health care coverage. *None* were disabled, and 80% were cancer patients.

Oregon's law also taught us another critical lesson: Although 246 Oregonians chose to use Oregon's compassionate law, another 120 patients went through the medical and legal process, purchased the necessary prescription, and then chose to die naturally—not using the medicine.

The defining issue was *choice* and having options: More than anything that is the human message of this law, it is that at the end of one's life to have some sense of self-control, some self-determination. Oregon is proud of the flawless way our law has worked and the end-of-life choices available to our citizens that allow them *true* death with dignity. As noted in an editorial in the *San Francisco Chronicle* a few months ago, "Where politics and religion have created a passionate debate, the government should remember who's really involved—real people with terminal illnesses who, through this law, can find some sense of peace and comfort in knowing that they have a choice."

Oregon looks forward to having the California legislature take positive action on their Compassionate Choices bill and to be able to offer the same choice for dignified, caring, pain-free deaths to terminally ill Californians, a choice that Oregonians have experienced for the past eight years.

*[**Note:** In 2015, California's legislature passed their End of Life Option Act by a healthy bipartisan margin. Governor Jerry Brown signed the bill into law.]*

Former Governor Barbara Roberts speaks at a press conference in Washington State, offering her support for passage of Washington's Death with Dignity law.

Speech Nineteen

COMPASSION AND CHOICES

Seattle, Washington — Summer 2007

I AM HONORED TODAY to speak with you on a subject very close to my heart. I have had a close connection to Oregon's Death with Dignity law for many years. I was Governor at the time of the passage of Oregon's Death with Dignity Act on the 1994 ballot. I publicly endorsed the measure as Governor and have closely followed its history in the years since. I have *never*, for a moment, regretted that endorsement.

This afternoon I want to share my experience and my state's experience with our landmark law and some of the benefits that have come to our state and our citizens. As Washington citizens, I believe Oregon's experience will be helpful as you consider a new law for Washington State.

While I make no pretense about being an expert on dying, I must confess I've had far more experience with death in the last two decades than anyone would want. In that time, I've buried my husband, my former husband, both of my parents, my younger sister who was my only sibling, plus my two best friends. And of this, I am certain: Life is a terminal condition. It will come to each of us.

The state of Oregon and its citizens have recognized that reality and have worked to bring dignity, support, caring, and pain management to the dying process.

Oregonians have taken death out of the closet and we have found that nondenial and openness bring more choice and more comfort to those at life's end.

Over the years, I have come to strongly believe that dying is more difficult in a culture of *denial;* grieving is more *painful* and *lonely* in a *society of silence.* My husband, state Senator Frank Roberts, was diagnosed with metastasized cancer in 1992 and given a year to live. He opted against any further treatment. I was Oregon's Governor at the time and Frank continued to serve in the Oregon Senate. Frank decided he was not ready to go public with his diagnosis. For over six months, we both remained silent about his impending death.

When Frank felt his health waning and his legislative duties required him to share his condition, he spoke publicly about his diagnosis and his decision to avoid any further treatment. For Frank and for me that public openness turned out to be a huge relief and the beginning of a chance to talk about some of the choices we had made. Across the state, the press began writing stories about hospice. Frank talked about choosing "quality-of-life" over the difficult cancer treatment that might prolong his life for a few weeks. We talked openly about the fact that Frank was dying. Frank and I even talked about "do not resuscitate" orders—that were soon posted in our home, in the car, and in Frank's office. Soon, there was no denial for us—or for our state.

That interminable 1993 legislative session, Frank's final session, ended in early August [Frank had worked until the end of the session] and Frank went on oxygen only four days later. He died on Halloween, at home in the governor's residence, under hospice care. He died as he lived, always trying to make the world a better place—in this case, demonstrating that terminal patients still had some end-of-life choices.

A year later, when the initiative petition reached the ballot, Oregon voters passed the Death with Dignity Act, which allowed physician-assisted death. Many people felt that the public way Frank and I handled his dying process played a role in that ballot success. And whether people support or oppose

Oregon's Death with Dignity Act, no one can deny the impact it has had on end-of-life issues in my state.

Now, let me give you a sense of that time period in Oregon in the 1990s. There were two, heavily-financed statewide campaigns. There were constant debates, television and radio ads, newspaper articles, and speeches. It was the biggest political issue happening in the state. Oregon voters became the best-informed Americans in any of our fifty states on the subjects of dying, pain medication, advance directives, and hospice care. With this expanded knowledge, more and more patients and their families expected difficult health matters to result—*not* in miracles—but in a *clear* diagnosis and prognosis. Since many physicians see death as a defeat and are reluctant to give up on aggressive treatments, newly informed patients were demanding more clarity and honesty from their physicians.

And that takes me back to Oregon's Death with Dignity law, which is about *truth* and *support* at the end of life. After ten years' experience with our law in Oregon and attempting to encourage similar laws in other states, it takes little analysis to know that the American public has moved ahead of its legislative bodies on their expectations for personal end-of-life choices. Recent polling across the nation has revealed and reinforced those citizen expectations. And now Washington state could definitely become a leader in the national end-of-life choice for its citizens.

However, without a doubt, part of the job is one of *education*. Oregon has an important story to tell to the rest of this nation about being informed on this issue. With the passage and implementation of the Oregon's Death with Dignity Act, end-of-life choices began to change in Oregon. Hospice use has increased notably with high quality hospice care now available in *every* county in our state. Today, Oregon has one of the highest-hospice uses in the country. More citizens in Oregon die at home than die in hospitals. For families and patients, this change has given them the caring and gentle exits they seek.

Since our law passed, Oregon's use of much-needed pain medication for terminal patients is one of the highest in the nation. It has become clear that the vastly improved pain management has allowed more quality time for patients and their families.

Now, in terms of perspective on the use of Oregon's law, let me share one more important issue: Personal control and choice. Often, I speak to audiences both in my own state and across the nation—hospice groups, hospital staffs, cancer groups, senior citizen organizations—and I have learned that more than costs and more than pain, the *biggest issue* for the terminally ill is loss of personal control, loss of choice. They want to have self-determination at the end of life. That is clearly evidenced by knowing that in addition to the 246 Oregonians who have died using Oregon's law in the first eight years, an additional 390 patients went through the *entire* legal and medical process, purchased the medication, and then opted *not* to use the prescription. The issue for them was *choice.*

More than *anything,* that is the human message of this law. This should not be a political issue but rather a human issue of self-determination and personal choice.

Oregon's law, with its safeguards, its careful implementation, its detailed reporting, its outcomes, and a decade of experience, offers other states the workable and *"tested"* model they can replicate with confidence for their own citizens. I urge Washington state, our neighbor, to take that step.

*[**Note:** The voters of Washington State passed their Death with Dignity law in November 2008, becoming the second state to do so. The ballot measure was approved by 59% of voters.]*

Speech Twenty
TESTIMONY TO VERMONT SENATE
HEALTH AND WELFARE COMMITTEE
Montpelier, Vermont — January 2013

MADAM CHAIR, MEMBERS OF THE COMMITTEE:

I am Barbara Roberts, Oregon's Governor from 1991 to 1995. During that time, Oregon's Death with Dignity Act was approved on our statewide ballot in 1994. As Governor, I publicly endorsed the measure and have remained strongly supportive of end-of-life choices in all the years since.

I am pleased to be before your Senate Health and Welfare Committee today. In both 2006 and 2007, I testified before your House Human Services Committee on the Death with Dignity bill then under consideration in Vermont.

As you may know, Oregon's law has *twice* been on the ballot for the decision of our voters: the first time by initiative petition in 1994 and the second time by legislative referral. The 1994 petition measure passed by 51% of the voters. The legislature's identical referral in 1997, passed with the voters' reaffirmation of 61%.

Then, and now, Oregon's citizens have continued to send a strong message of support for our state's end-of-life law. And across America, ongoing polling continually reinforces citizen expectations and wishes about personal end-of-life options.

In Oregon, where the law has been in effect for sixteen years, Oregon families and patients gained a greater understanding

Oregon Governor Barbara Roberts and Vermont Governor Madeleine Kunin were both strong supporters of their respective states' Death with Dignity laws. Oregon's law passed in 1994 and Vermont's law passed in 2013.

of medical matters, treatment choices, and end-of-life options. They soon had expanded expectations of their own medical providers. Far beyond simply the Death with Dignity law, the understanding of end of life changed in Oregon. For instance, use of hospice was increased notably. High-quality hospice care was soon available in *every one* of Oregon's thirty-six counties. Today, Oregon has one of the highest-hospice uses in the nation.

Since our law passed, Oregon's much-needed pain medication for terminal patients has resulted in a vastly improved pain management system across Oregon. This improved pain management is more realistic and more caring. It has even prevented a number of violent suicides when patients suffered from under-treated pain. "Kinder and gentler" accurately describe end of life in Oregon. Even our medical schools have improved and expanded end-of-life training for doctors preparing to serve terminal patients in our state.

However, if I might, there is a short but important discussion point I'd like to share with you as you consider the Death with Dignity law here in Vermont. In the exchanges and debates on the Death with Dignity proposals, in a number of states there is a phrase I've heard a number of times regarding citizens with disabilities and the Death with Dignity laws proposed. That phrase is *"slippery slope."* So let me be very clear: this phrase has *no place* in the discussion of this piece of legislation.

I have spent over forty years as a disability rights activist. My older son is autistic and my political fight in 1971 for his right to a public-school education was my first entry into the political process. From citizen advocate to governor, I have continued my strong commitment to members of the disability community.

I also experienced the challenges of a husband who was confined to a wheelchair for over seven years. At the time of my husband's death in 1993, Senator Frank Roberts was the longest-serving member of the Oregon legislature. He proved that his disability did not stand in the way of the remarkable contributions he made to public policy in Oregon.

So, let me state emphatically, I would *never* support a law that was harmful, even threatening, to individuals with disabilities. And let me add that in Oregon, after fifteen years of actual experience with this law, *no person* with a pre-existing disability has used the Oregon law.

For anyone to raise the issue that Death with Dignity endangers those with disabilities has *no basis* in fact or in Oregon's fifteen-year experience. This argument is both *baseless* and *unkind.* It raises fears and anxiety in the disability community that, in my opinion, are forms of emotional abuse. This baseless issue has *absolutely no merit.*

So, that said, let me take a minute or two to lay out some real facts about Oregon's experience with this law. In Oregon, about 30,000 of our people die annually. In the fifteen years from 1998 to 2012, approximately 450,000 Oregonians have died. In those same years, a total of 1,050 people had prescriptions written under the Death with Dignity law. Of those, 673 patients have used the mediations to end their life. These numbers tell us two important things: One, Oregon's Death with Dignity law has been used sparingly; and two, every patient who has the prescription knows they retain the option for dying *with* or *without* the medication.

Fifteen years; 450,000 Oregon deaths; 1,050 prescriptions written; 673 terminal patients choosing their own end-of-life path. There is comfort in self-determination.

Predictions and campaign allegations of overuse and tragedy have *long ago* been discredited. Oregonians have used the law with careful consideration and with full adherence to both the letter and the spirit with which the law was designed. Oregon families have, over the years, shared beautiful and moving accounts of compassion, dignity, and gentle exits.

A quick summary of our 2012 experience reflects once again many of the facts we have found at year's end over the history of our law.

In 2012, Oregon's Death with Dignity reports showed that 67% were patients 65 years of age or older; 75% had cancer;

97% died at home; 97% were enrolled in hospice; and 100% had some form of health care insurance. The 77 deaths included 39 males and 38 females.

In the state of Washington, their four years of experience with the law have closely mirrored Oregon's. Their numbers are a little higher—but that reflects the larger population numbers in Washington state.

Oregon is proud of the flawless way our law has worked in practice; our state government's careful and detailed reporting system, the professional work and support of our medical and pharmaceutical communities, the strong partnership with Oregon hospice, and an electorate that retains its protective support of the law.

I encourage your Senate committee to bring that same positive outcome to the citizens of Vermont. I fully trust that if you bring this caring option to your state, years from now you will look back on this decision, as I do today, with pride and gratitude for your state's leadership and for the role you played in moving this compassionate agenda.

*[**Note:** In 2013, the Vermont House and Senate passed the state's Death with Dignity law and Governor Peter Shumlin signed it into law. Vermont's bill had been under legislative consideration for more than a decade.]*

Section Six

A Voice for
the Environment

*Governor Barbara Roberts meeting with President Bill Clinton and
Vice President Al Gore at the Northwest Forest Summit in April 1993
during the tumultuous spotted owl crisis.*

Speech Twenty-One

ELEVEN-YEAR RETROSPECTIVE
OF THE CLINTON FOREST PLAN

Corvallis, Oregon — November 2005

Introduction: Few policy issues in my life come anywhere near the challenges I experienced as Oregon's Governor in handling the spotted owl crisis. The federal listing of the spotted owl as an endangered species created an economic, environmental, and political disruption that *rocked* the state of Oregon.

When I received a speaking invitation fifteen years later to return to the scene of that crisis, to relive the anger, stress, and alienation of that political nightmare, I almost declined the offer. Yet, the four-day conference focused on looking back at that crisis and the trauma over managing the ecosystems of our Northwest forests, I needed to rethink my answer. This was a rare opportunity to express my policy views, both then and now, plus add some important recollections of lessons learned and history in the making.

The day of my 2005 speech in Corvallis, Oregon, the audience and participants were both impressive and representative of a slice of that history. Scientists, academics, former federal leaders, environmental leaders, legal experts, biologists, industry leaders, and labor experts were in attendance.

When I stepped up to the podium and stepped back into the Northern Spotted Owl controversy, it again felt like a quagmire of policy and politics, closed-minds, and open wounds. Even after fifteen years, the emotional pain returned.

And when the speech was finished, I experienced the sense of closing a tumultuous chapter of my life. The success or failure of how we've managed our Oregon forests will not be fully evaluated for decades. However, perhaps the willingness to think long term and to accept the facts that science presents to us about our forest ecosystems will give Oregon a respectful future for this valuable resource.

As Governor, I did my best to move Oregon in that direction and I am *scarred, but grateful* for my moment in the sun.

Good Afternoon,

When Ward Armstrong [timber industry guru] called several weeks ago and asked if I would join your conference today and share some remarks on my experiences with forest policy matters during my governorship, I was tempted to tell him, "No."

It seemed like reliving a bad marriage where divorce feels like success!

Ward assured me I wouldn't have to do any preparation, just come and "chat" with you about the spotted owl, the timber crisis, the political and policy fallout, and what "fun" it was to be governor at the height of that controversy.

My calendar has been a scheduling nightmare for the past two months and I considered following Ward's advice about showing up and simply *chatting* with you. But once I began thinking about the issues and that period of environmental, economic, and political *disruption*, I knew that I really needed to lay a little foundation. I needed to set my remarks in the context of the early 1990s and my personal and political experiences. So, let me start with seven statements that I'll elaborate on, but for now, they will get us started with our *little chat:*

#1. It ain't easy being green (from Kermit the frog).

#2. Jobs vs. the environment is a false choice.

#3. An oath of office comes with a commitment to the law.

#4. Neither nature nor the economy are *static systems.*

#5. "Quick fixes" seldom fix anything.

#6. Political courage is *not* inexpensive.

#7. Science can be a harsh *taskmaster.*

Let me now put some details on those seven statements.

1. It ain't easy being green.

During the 1990 governor's race in Oregon, the Northern Spotted Owl was listed under the federal Endangered Species Act. It was like the Northwest had been hit by a terrorist attack—not so much the instant damage in this case but the *instant hysteria.* I was running for governor and the press immediately wanted to know my reaction. And I was clear: I *supported* the federal Endangered Species Act. Talk about the you-know-what hitting the fan. *Never* in the history of Oregon had *any* governor been elected without the support of the timber industry. Was it possible for *me* to be that *exception?*

This issue was the most divisive, polarizing issue I'd ever witnessed in my state. I'd been involved with the controversies of sex education, gay rights, and abortion, but this issue totally divided Oregon's citizens. There was literally *no middle ground.*

2. Jobs vs. the environment is a false choice.

An extensive state-by-state study done in 1994 showed that the top dozen states in the U.S. ranked by strict environmental laws and rules, also ranked as the top states *economically.* Conversely, states judged lowest on environmental standards also ranked at the *bottom* economically. Oregon was in the top dozen states, environmentally and economically. But that said, the spotted owl and the Northwest salmon species were ranked as causing the most expansive impacts of any listed species under the Endangered Species Act. Our challenges under the federal law were more complex and costly in every sense than in any other area in the nation.

3. An oath of office comes with a commitment to the law.

When you raise your hand and take the oath of office as governor, you pledge to abide by *both* the state and federal laws. Not just some laws—*all* the laws. And not only was I obligated to that legal requirement, so was my administration and all of state government. And as I'll share in a couple of minutes, I believed so was the *federal* government.

4. Neither nature nor the economy are static systems.

During the 1990 campaign for governor, I delivered a speech to the Northwest Forestry Association—not exactly a friendly audience for me at the time. I shared with them a little research I'd uncovered. I described an in-depth, 1936 research report done by the Oregon State University Planning Board. The Oregon State report warned of *over* harvesting and *under* replanting, and said if the levels of harvest continued at the 1936 levels, within fifty years there would be a timber shortage crisis in Oregon. Well, as you might imagine, that report was soon gathering dust. The industry, the legislature, and the state government leadership were unwilling to "bite the bullet" then, and left us with the harvest supply issue we now face in the 1990s *and beyond.*

Once listed, the spotted owl immediately became the culprit. It even made the front cover of *Time Magazine.* But the real culprit was our unwillingness to respond to that *first* 1936 report that advocated for *sustained harvesting.*

I had watched the crisis happening over many years. I come from a small timber community in Yamhill County. When I was in high school, we had a number of active, smaller mills, lots of logging trucks, and a huge plywood mill. By the time I was running for governor, most of the mills were gone, the plywood operation was closed, and those trucks were hauling *smaller* logs for *longer* distances for *less profit.*

By then, Oregon and Washington were also exporting huge ships full of logs offshore and the processing jobs were happening in Asia instead of the Pacific Northwest. Plus, the big mills here that were still operating were more and more computerized, needing fewer and fewer workers. The industry was clearly *not* static, but it was moving toward a *bleak*, long-term future—an unsustainable future. The spotted owl was simply an *indicator species* after decades of short-term thinking.

5. Quick-fixes" seldom fix anything.

When nature, the environment, sustainability, and leadership are in play, "quick-fixes" offer a formula for long-term *failure*. I'll leave it at that right now. It perhaps, says it all.

6. Political courage is not inexpensive.

Because I adhered to the law, spoke honestly about finding and developing biologically sound, legally defensible harvest levels, and species protection, I was definitely the "bad guy." The timber industry and the workers and residents from timber communities assumed I didn't understand their industry, their crisis, and cared nothing about them or their future.

I knew I couldn't help those communities if the debate ended up for years in courtrooms and legal hearings. The industry would be tied up with uncertainty and the inability to plan or invest with any confidence. We weren't going to fix the policy or political landscape with demonstrations, name calling, or bumper strips about fried owls.

We had to have a plan. The law *required* a recovery plan for the owl. The recovery team began its work, but politics and an overall refusal by many to face the reality of our situation, slowed the recovery team's work. Finally, in early 1992 the team produced a viable recovery plan.

But here we ran into a new issue; U.S. Secretary of Interior Manuel Lujan simply put the plan on the shelf. After months of work by both state and federal leaders, he ignored the plan and *refused* to implement it. He tried to *outflank* science and the law by pushing forty-four Bureau of Land Management timber sales forward and granting exemptions to the new ESA owl protections.

This basically moved the decision forward to the Endangered Species Committee, called the "God Squad." This was clearly grandstanding and it was outside the scope of the law. So, I *sued* the Secretary of Interior for failing to respond to the findings of his own spotted owl recovery team. I *challenged* his right to put the "God Squad" into action and of shortcutting the recovery plan and the law. Well, talk about a political *explosion!*

The industry was furious. Timber and mill workers were hopping mad. Timber community legislators of *both* parties were holding press conferences right and left. I could feel the heat!

We had to have a recovery plan in place if we were ever going to get back into the *woods* instead of the courts. Lujan's actions were making things worse, not better. I was taking hits from every direction, with a few important exceptions. On February 29, 1992, *The Oregonian* newspaper wrote an editorial on my actions as governor and the reaction to my lawsuit: "This is a realistic state response. It addresses the situation squarely. Yet, for suggesting it, Governor Roberts has incurred open hostility.

"Actually, the American Forest Resource lobby group's opposition to federal policies and industry positions that, while supposedly sensitive to timber jobs and communities, have been disastrous for them. The refusal to face the threat to the spotted owl directly and promptly, not anything the governor has done, is what has produced the chaos in the federal forests."

Other newspapers statewide voiced similar views. On February 27, 1992, *The Daily Astorian* noted: "If Governor Roberts is guilty of anything, it is speaking the truth about the Bureau of Land Management and Interior Secretary Manuel Lujan....Lujan and the BLM are breaking the law. The day of reckoning has now arrived. People who think that moment can be put off by getting one more, illegal federal exemption are kidding themselves. They are peddling illusion."

But in spite of such editorial support, this statewide flap grew and resulted in a recall petition being filed against me, the first time a recall had ever been filed against an Oregon governor.

The recall failed to garner enough signatures to reach the ballot. Two more recalls were later filed, each one receiving fewer signatures than the one before. All three recalls failed, but the lawsuit against the Secretary of Interior was a *legal slam dunk* for me. Lujan had clearly breached the ESA and the use of the "God Squad." He had also *delayed* the process of implementing a recovery plan.

Yet, during these turbulent times, it was hard to tell the *winners* from the *losers* in Oregon. Where we needed solutions, we got nothing but delays. Where we needed collaboration and ideas, we got only conflict and monkey wrenches. So, the state government moved to working on our *state* forests, like the Elliot Forest in Coos County, using solid science and creative ideas for harvest and recovery that eventually allowed us to harvest on the Elliot Forest. The State Land Board, which I chaired, was determined we could do it successfully and we did.

When Bill Clinton was elected President in 1992, his new administration moved forward toward the spotted owl recovery plan for the Northwest and injected massive financial support for the timber communities and timber workers, some in need of job retraining. I carried the details of the Clinton Forest plan to Springfield, Coos Bay, Roseburg, Medford, and other timber-dependent communities. I was not really sure anybody was listening; everyone seemed only willing to turn back the clock.

I understood that the issues were much broader than the spotted owl and they had been decades in arriving at this *point of crisis.* I also knew I was seen as the person who stood in the way of the future of the industry. In truth, I was the person trying to make certain the industry *had* a long-term future in my state. I really believed, then and now, in sustainable forest management. And I have the scar tissue to prove I stood up for that belief, plus adhering to the state and federal laws.

And finally, statement number seven:

7. Science can be a harsh taskmaster.

Remember that old television line from a margarine commercial: "You can't fool Mother Nature." *Well, you can't.*

We can each put our own "spin" on the research and reports we fund or support, but unless the science is 100% accurate and truly defensible, our "slant" will come home to haunt us. No matter who funds our research and no matter who pays our salary, we owe today and we owe the future the most accurate and honest science we can assemble. To do anything less than that is dishonorable and unprofessional.

Let us not try to *fool* Mother Nature!

Participants in this amazing conference have a wonderful opportunity to spend four days examining a remarkable time in Northwest history and the decade since. I've lived a portion of that history, *up close* and personal. I wouldn't want to do it *again*, but I don't know that I'd do it differently. Part of the role of a leader is to help people face change. I played that role, often standing in front of a big red bulls-eye to deliver my leadership decisions.

But someone has to be there in the tough times and I never regretted that it was me. I come from Oregon Trail pioneer stock and my heritage should have made me strong enough to do the work of Oregon's future and I believe it did!

Speech Twenty-Two
Bureau of Land Management and the Public Lands Foundation
Baker City, Oregon — August 2018

Introduction: This final speech in my book of advocacy speeches is the most current of the twenty-two speeches I have included. Delivered in 2018, the speech is about our state's environment, our history, and the role *collaboration* has played in preserving both.

I was contacted months in advance of this speech with an invitation to attend a conference conducted by the Federal Bureau of Land Management and the Public Lands Foundation. This event is called the "Student Congress" and approximately fifty college students from every part of the nation are selected to participate. These fifty students would make up the "student body" for a five-day experience in learning about the importance of protecting and conserving our nation's public lands.

I was asked to help the Student Congress begin to understand the value of these public lands, the huge variety in the kinds of lands they represent, and some of the threats to the preservation and health of these public assets. The organizers wanted me to share the depth of collaboration that is needed to save special sites for future generations. They hoped my stories of Oregon experiences would inspire these students, even to the point of making career decisions, perhaps one day joining public land organizations.

So, my mission was before me: Inform, educate, inspire, recruit.

My environmental credentials in Oregon during my more than thirty years as an elected official and public servant, were positive and wide-ranging. I had actively promoted the closure of Oregon's only nuclear power plant. I supported the federal Endangered Species Act, and worked to protect river water quality, clean air, and responsible agriculture. I had taken leadership at the local and state level to advance mass transit. As Governor, I had stepped up for estuary protection, responsible forestry practices, and curtailed mining processes using heap leaching. But this speech request was focused on public lands and public waterways. I asked myself, *Do I have a story to tell that would meet the expectations of my host organizations and the hopes of the students selected for this high-level conference?*

The following speech is the result of my work to answer that question.

⌐——⌐

THANK YOU AND GOOD EVENING.

I am particularly pleased to welcome the members of this year's Student Congress to the state of Oregon. And I thank BLM and the Public Lands Foundation for giving me such a great excuse to be here in Baker City.

My great-great grandparents arrived in Oregon on the Oregon Trail in 1853, passing through what is now Baker County. I never arrive here without feeling the stirrings as a descendent of the Oregon Trail—one of the largest human migrations in history.

This far-eastern part of my state offers vast plains, white-water rivers, deep canyons, and shear, rugged mountains. It is a photographer's delight, an unending recreational playground, and a biologist's gigantic laboratory.

Barbara Roberts campaigning in Eastern Oregon in 1984, traveling to every county in the state to reach a diverse population of constituents.

And for members of this year's Student Congress, Baker City has now become a highly unique classroom with a curriculum, rare and exploratory.

So, for me, the questions are: What can I add to your student knowledge base here tonight? How can I expand your appreciation for public lands—both federal and state-managed lands? What experiences can I share with you that will help explain what complex environmental collaboration really looks and feels like?

I believe I can best set the stage for the experiences I want to share with you by putting a little context in place to enhance my storytelling. So, here's that context.

I was elected governor of Oregon in November 1990. I became my state's first woman governor and one of the first ten female governors in America. The Northern Spotted Owl was listed as an endangered species during that 1990 campaign season while I was running for governor. I supported the Endangered Species Act [ESA]; my opponent opposed the owl's listing. But in spite of the controversy of my position, I was the first governor ever elected in Oregon without the support of the timber industry—Oregon's largest industry at that time.

And while ESA listings usually have their share of controversy, the impact of the spotted owl listing in the forests of Oregon, Washington, and Northern California was beyond dramatic! This was not some little fish in a landlocked lake in the Midwest. The spotted owl listing impacted tens-of-thousands of prime timber acreage that also housed the nesting sites for the endangered owls. This situation was totally polarizing. There was *no* middle ground.

The federal courts and Oregon courts faced the impact of dozens of lawsuits challenging the listing of the spotted owl as major forests were shut down, as many sawmills closed, and as workers by the thousands faced unemployment in the woods and the mills. It became the prime example of the often, mislabeled story of "the environment vs. the economy." It was the battle of verifiable science vs. the timber industry's long history in the Northwest.

For me, facing reality and the federal law was about personal fortitude and about proposing tough solutions, and often about speaking to angry demonstrators and about acquiring "scar-tissue."

This was a notable backdrop for my four years as Oregon's governor. No easy answers. No quick fixes.

The federal law required a recovery plan for the owl. And finally, after months of work by both state and federal leaders and scientists, in early 1992 the recovery team produced a viable recovery plan. It was a huge step. I understood clearly that we had to have a recovery plan in place if we were ever going to get back in the woods instead of in the courts. And then, to my dismay, Secretary of Interior Manual Lujan simply put the long-awaited plan on the shelf. He pushed huge timber sales forward and granted exemptions to the new ESA owl protections.

So, *this* small-town girl from Oregon, *this* descendent of the Oregon Trail, *this* totally "pissed-off" governor of Oregon, sued the Secretary of the Interior of the United States—*and I won!*

Yet, frankly, during such turbulent times it is hard to tell the winners from the losers. Where we needed solutions, we got mostly delays. Where we needed collaboration and ideas, we got conflict and monkey wrenches. But out of such tough times I learned solid lessons.

The decisions we make, the actions we take, the long-term thinking we apply to the care of our public lands—all of these will set the stage for the environmental heritage we leave to generations yet unborn. With those lessons in mind—and my hopes that as governor I not only acted wisely for today, but made choices for what the Native American tribes define as the "next seven generations"—let me share some policy "war stories" about caring for some very special lands and waterways.

I am supposedly a retired public official, but I have difficulty getting my state to recognize the "retired" part. In 2015, the Oregon legislature created a special, two-year task force to study a huge and very complex matter; I was asked to chair the task force and bring our report and our recommendations back to the 2017 legislature.

Here was our challenge: The Willamette River in Oregon is 187 miles long. It meanders north through eight counties as it heads to the mighty Columbia River and the Pacific Ocean. Today, the river passes farms, vineyards, and towns as it moves through the rich valley acreage that borders the Willamette River. Without question, the most significant feature on this major river is the magnificent and powerful Willamette Falls that plunge down over forty-five feet from the river's surface as the river reaches the community site that once housed the first capitol of the Oregon Territory. The Willamette Falls were also a sacred gathering site for several Native tribes for centuries.

But in spite of the amazing history that surrounds Willamette Falls, there is a current challenge at that location on the river. Decades ago, as the Willamette River began to experience more and larger boats, these huge waterfalls impeded economic water traffic. This is the second largest waterfall in the continental United States and it is located near the center of what would normally be a major boat lane.

The early growth of the timber industry created an even more complicated challenge on the river as they began moving newly-cut logs, lashed together as huge rafts, to mill sites on the river bank. At this point, the federal government stepped in with a solution to this economic problem: They proposed and constructed an amazing locks system on the river, opening the river to boats, barges, and log rafts. That was 145 years ago.

The federal Army Corps of Engineers has owned and operated the Willamette Falls Locks since the 1870s. But at this point, the Corps had decided to decommission the locks, either disposing of them to another agency or permanently closing the locks and blocking navigation to the river above the falls. The Corps believes the locks are no longer needed for economic enhancement. Oregon sees the locks as vital to tourism, recreation, future commercial opportunities, and new economic and history-related projects.

So, at the request of my task force, the legislature created a new commission to directly negotiate with the Army Corps of Engineers. They must create a legal entity to repair, maintain, and operate the locks and to assume legal ownership of the property. There is a very tight timeline to find these answers. Oregon must act soon. We must present our decisions and our plans for ownership to the Corps soon.

I met and testified before the new Willamette Falls Locks Commission last month. I was clear that Oregon couldn't let this opportunity slip through our fingers. As I looked at the leaders around the commission table and assembled in that room, I understood that there was the talent and dedication available to tackle this huge assignment. We clearly had the expertise ready!

We needed ideas and total commitment. A multi-issue project with massive complexity. What an incredible case study this will one day be for some student, professor, or writer. I await the outcome and am grateful for the two-year opportunity I was given to help launch this extraordinary proposal.

This Willamette Falls Locks project is an important reminder that while this Student Congress is focused on public *lands,* many of the same principles and challenges face our public *waterways.* Here is another perfect example:

During my four years as Oregon Governor, I led and saw an important success on a mainly rural river near the California border in southern Oregon. The local county commission began planning a hydro project on the last eleven-mile stretch that remained free-flowing on the Klamath River. California would buy the electrical production and the county would earn the profits. However, the river would be permanently injured; a Native American tribal burial ground would be submerged; and a great fishing stretch of the river would disappear.

I opposed the project and began the huge effort to gain designation as a National Wild and Scenic River for the Klamath River in Oregon. I knew that designation would prohibit the construction of the proposed hydro facility on that beautiful, wild river. I lobbied Secretary of Interior Bruce Babbitt, himself a Westerner who respected the importance of the health and vitality of America's rivers.

Finally, after three years of effort to save the Klamath River, during my final month as Oregon's governor, the designation for the Klamath River was approved. The hydro project was shelved; the Native American burial ground was protected; and fly fishermen still respect the great fishing available on this wild river. On this 50th anniversary of the federal Wild and Scenic Rivers Act, I am very proud of the role I played in adding this special Oregon waterway to that list of protected rivers.

However, unlike the three-year story of the Klamath River, my next accounting of creating an environmental legacy spanned decades, brought hundreds of advocates together, and dozens of government jurisdictions played big roles. It went all the way to the President of the United States. Here is that story:

This amazing site is the Columbia Gorge where the mighty Columbia River runs, creating a canyon with steep dramatic walls of exposed volcanic rock. This gorge and this river create the border between the states of Oregon and Washington. At the end of the Ice Age, the great Missoula Floods cut these towering rock walls that exist today. This amazing gorge has supported human habitation for over 13,000 years. It has provided a transportation corridor for thousands of years. In fact, in 1805 this river route was used by explorers Lewis & Clark to reach the Pacific Ocean.

In the early 1900s, the hidden beauty of the Columbia River Gorge was discovered by the public when the first major paved highway was opened through the Gorge. Naturalists, photographers, and civic-minded leaders began to advocate for protecting the area. Developers and entrepreneurs saw the great beauty and its proximity to the city of Portland and pushed schemes for heavy development. That push and pull between conservation and development continued for decades.

By 1980, the pressure from both camps intensified. At the same time, the National Parks Service was conducting a study of the Columbia Gorge. One of the recommendations from that study was to establish the Columbia River Gorge as a National Scenic Area.

That recommendation and that 1980 timing were a perfect match to a newly-forming group named the Committee to Save the Gorge. The civic leader of that new committee was a Portland woman, an active backpacker, wildflower enthusiast, and lover of the Columbia Gorge. Nancy Russell's thirty-eight members on the committee were mostly members of her Portland Garden Club, and believe me, they were determined and dedicated. And that was clearly going to be necessary if they were going to build support for a congressionally designated, bistate scenic area.

That challenge got even more difficult as the new Reagan administration took office and the new Secretary of the Interior James Watt brought his pro-development attitude to the Department of the Interior.

By the spring of 1981, Nancy Russell's committee had become the newly-named Friends of the Columbia Gorge. They were becoming a notable political force. Their steering committee included three former governors; Tom McCall and Bob Straub of Oregon and Dan Evans of Washington State. They also had elected local government leaders and legislators from both sides of the river on their supporters list. And they had the efforts and outreach coming from Washington, D.C., and the work of Oregon's U.S. Senator Mark Hatfield and Oregon Congressman Les AuCoin.

The journey to success was long and complex. The work continued. Outreach to congressional members expanded. Newspaper endorsements grew in both states. Finally, on November 17, 1986, almost six years to the day that the Friends of the Columbia Gorge announced its formation, President Ronald Regan signed the Columbia River Gorge National Scenic Area Act.

Oregon Senator Mark Hatfield, who witnessed the signing of the Gorge Act, reported with a smile that Reagan signed the bill with one hand while holding his nose with the other. A joke? I'm not sure! But what I am sure of is where thirty-two years of scenic area protection and dedication has led the Northwest. Today, the Columbia River Gorge National Scenic Area protects nearly 293,000 acres of forests, trails, waterfalls, parks, and historical sites. There are over eighty miles of the beautiful Columbia River in that scenic area. In those eighty miles, the Columbia Gorge transitions between temperate rain forests to dry grasslands.

The area is known for its high concentration of waterfalls, with more than ninety on the Oregon side of the Gorge, alone. The most notable is the 540-foot Multnomah Falls. There are approximately 200 miles of trails in the Gorge and they are maintained by the National Forest Service, Oregon and Washington Park Services, and Friends of the Gorge.

The National Scenic Area Act for the Gorge also created a legal governing commission that includes representatives for both states, six counties, four Native American tribes, and the U.S. Forest Service. The Columbia River Gorge Commission works to implement a regional management plan to protect and provide for the enhancement of the scenic, natural, cultural, and recreational resources of the Gorge. That's their job!

As the official Gorge Commission's work has continued and expanded over the last three decades, the Friends of the Gorge organization has also grown. Friends now has more than 7,000 paid members, and their love and caring for this scenic treasure is demonstrated in many remarkable ways.

In 2018, the Friends organization completed a campaign goal for their land conservation effort called "Preserve the Wonder." They reached a $5.5 million goal to purchase the most scenic landscapes, crucial wildlife habitat, and best recreational and trail opportunities available in the Gorge. The seven sites and 422 acres that Friends purchased have added to the protected wonders in the Columbia River Gorge Scenic Area.

The Columbia Gorge is a popular destination for hiking, fishing, watersports, sightseeing, and photography. Recreation-influenced economies in Hood River and Wasco Counties on the Oregon side of the Gorge have allowed them to have the lowest unemployment rates in Oregon. On the Washington side of the Columbia River, there is a thriving wine industry that adds to the economy, plus its beautiful vineyards enhance the scenic aspect of the Gorge.

In 2009, I had the special opportunity to be appointed by the governor to serve for two years on the Gorge Commission. It was hard work and heavy-duty decision-making, but I felt privileged to carry on the vision that emerged from Nancy Russell and the Portland Garden Club "ladies' in 1980. What a citizen legacy! I have also been an enthusiastic long-time member of Friends of the Gorge.

My life and my work have given me so many opportunities to witness the dramatic beauty and grandeur of the lands and waterways of my state. From the Pacific Ocean on Oregon's western border where our beaches are owned by our citizens, to the prairies, the plains, the forests, and the wheat fields of eastern Oregon where public and private ownership create a crazy quilt of land management, I am grateful for the chances

I've had to impact some of those lands and rivers. I did that with the Klamath River designation. And working jointly with the governor of Washington state, we saved a river estuary on my last day as governor. Plus, my work on the Willamette Falls Locks project continues.

But before I close, I want to focus on one other aspect of protection and preservation. That issue is saving and caring for our history, because where we have land, we have people. And where we have people, there is history. And since we are here tonight in Baker City with its remarkable Oregon Trail Interpretive Center, a place where the history of the Oregon Trail comes alive, I want us to share some of that history.

History is not meant to sit on an old shelf gathering dust. History is to think about, talk about, and learn from. For instance, Oregon has unique collections of firsthand accounts of the Oregon Trail experience. That amazing six-month trek, long and difficult, was captured in hundreds of diaries written almost entirely by the women and teenage girls of those wagon trains. Many of those diaries are housed at the Oregon Historical Society in Portland; some are here in Baker City. They recorded the challenges, the births, the deaths, the changing landscapes, the hardships, and the hopes. They preserved the history of that massive migration West for all the generations that followed.

Firsthand accounts have an ability to not only record history, not only teach and educate, but to transport the reader back to another time, another place, another experience. The Interpretive Center in Baker City has taken those written accounts and transformed them into a visual, lifelike walk through history. The 'walk' is educational, moving, and very importantly, accurate.

So often, television and movies have depicted tales of the Oregon Trail with whole families riding in the covered wagons and constant battles between the pioneers and the Indian tribes. Those films are often more about invention than reality. In reality, much of the Oregon Trail story is about *partings*. Of course, there were dreams of reaching the so-called "Eden of the West," but in order to make that happen, there were many sad partings.

Imagine leaving behind your parents and siblings, never expecting to see them again. And for six months they walked, not rode, but *walked* across this country. Along that great trail they observed the continuous partings; cast-iron stoves, too heavy to pull any longer, left beside the trail, along with beds, and trunks, and books, and paintings, and cradles, and most painful of all, the grave sites for the dead—hundreds and hundreds of them. The Oregon Trail has been described as the longest graveyard in the history of man. Painful partings with no chance to return.

Whenever I think of the sadness of this story, I am reminded of another important element of this difficult journey. Today, we might describe it as teamwork. Even though each covered wagon was like an island unto itself, carrying all its supplies and needs, once these moving islands became part of a wagon train, they became almost a commune—sharing hunting and fishing catches, carpentry skills, animal knowledge, and medical needs. They birthed and buried together. They played and prayed together. And they accepted into their wagons the children orphaned on the trial.

These pioneers often began their journey as strangers from different states, even different countries. But they formed bonds of friendship and necessity that helped them, not only reach their Promise Land, but to then become founders of farms, schools, towns, churches, and businesses. There are so many lessons to be learned from those pioneers about teamwork, collaboration, and not giving up until you reach your goal. And the dreamers, collaborators, fundraisers, builders, historians, and citizens who created the Oregon Trail Interpretive Center have followed the teachings of those brave pioneers. In turn, the Bureau of Land Management, the U.S. Forest Service, the U.S. Department of the Interior, the state of Oregon, Baker County, business and citizen donors, foundations, even schoolchildren—they *all* dreamed, they worked, and they built!

So, today you can stand on the hillside next to this hall of history and gaze down on the still-existing wagon ruts that scar the land below after more than 165 years since the pioneers traversed this historic trail.

As I said earlier, "Where we have land, we have had people. And where there have been people, there is history."

And each of you has an opportunity to impact that history. Our work and our voices matter as protectors, caregivers, scientists, and advocates of our lands, our rivers, our forests, our canyons and prairies, and our historical sites.

Students, you will take away from this Student Congress new knowledge, new understanding, and new potential for being the workers and voices of the future of our public lands.

That potential is in your hands.

Author's Reflections

As I come to the end of this book, I am reminded that life does not come with a built-in "Table of Contents."

Life comes with challenges and opportunities, with crossroads and detours.

Our role is to choose the path, to take the steps, and to design the map that will lead each of us to our journey's end.

I am grateful for the opportunities I've had to step forward for others. I feel gratitude for those who heard my voice and so often followed my lead.

I want this book to remind others that around every corner, life offers you an opportunity to take a hand, lift a spirit, warm a heart, touch a life.

I hope you have felt my commitment to others in the causes I have championed.

—Barbara Roberts
March 2022

Barbara K. Roberts

ABOUT THE AUTHOR

BARBARA ROBERTS was elected the 34th Governor of Oregon in 1990, becoming the first woman governor in her state and one of the first ten women governors in the nation. Previously, she held public office for twenty-four years, including ten years as a public-school board member, a community-college board member, a county commissioner, a state representative, and the first woman to serve as majority leader in the Oregon House of Representatives. In addition, Roberts was elected to two terms as Oregon Secretary of State (1984 to 1990), serving six years before her election as Governor.

Barbara Roberts is a native Oregonian and a fourth-generation descendant of 1853 Oregon Trail pioneers. Her father was a minister's son from Oregon and her mother was a farmer's daughter from Montana. Barbara and her sister, Pat, grew up in Sheridan, a small Oregon town with fewer than 2,000 people. Roberts describes her parents, Bob Hughey and Carmen Murray Hughey, as warm and caring, and she considered her father one of her greatest supporters. Her dad was proud of his two daughters and encouraged them to be active in school and the community.

At 18, Barbara married her high school boyfriend. As soon as she graduated from high school as class salutatorian, she moved to Texas where her husband was serving in the U.S. Air Force. Her first son, Michael Sanders, was born in Texas in 1956. Her younger son, Mark Sanders, was born in 1958 after her return to Oregon.

After sixteen years of marriage, a divorce left Barbara raising two sons as a single parent with no child support and a low-paying office job. As a result, her part-time college classes were no longer financially possible and she had to leave college.

When Barbara's son Mike was diagnosed with autism and school authorities would no longer accept him as a student, she knew she had to step up and advocate for him. So, Barbara began her active public service life as an unpaid, part-time, legislative advocate for children with disabilities. Six months later, she was successful in securing passage of one of the first special education laws in the nation that served children with emotional disorders. That first legislative win was the start of a long, notable, political career.

In 1974, Barbara married Frank Roberts, who was her state senator and political mentor. Frank became Barbara's biggest fan, eventually encouraging her to run for secretary of state and governor. In 1993, during her term as governor, Frank died of cancer. They had been happily married for twenty years.

Following her term as Oregon's governor, Barbara Roberts spent a decade in higher education administration focused on state and local government leadership. She served five years at Harvard's Kennedy School of Government, followed by five years at Portland State University's Hatfield School of Government in Oregon.

Among her many recognitions is the naming of the Oregon Department of Human Services Building in her honor and the Barbara Roberts High School in Salem. Governor Roberts was also awarded an Honorary Doctor of Laws from Willamette University, an Honorary Doctor of Letters from Portland State University, and an Honorary Doctor of Humane Letters from Western University College of Osteopathic Medicine. In addition, as part of *USA TODAY's* "Women of the Century," a 50-state national program recognizing trailblazing women in every state, Governor Roberts was named one of Oregon's ten "Women of the Century" in 2020.

Barbara Roberts is a published author with four books, including her autobiography, *Up the Capitol Steps: A Woman's March to the Governorship* (Oregon State University Press, 2011), and two editions of *Death Without Denial, Grief Without Apology* (NewSage Press, 2002 and 2016). With her latest book, *A Voice for Equity*, Roberts continues to be a vocal advocate for women's leadership, disability issues, LGBTQ+ rights, environmental concerns, and equality and dignity for *all* people.

Barbara Roberts lives in Portland, Oregon with her significant other, Don Nelson. She is a mother to two adult sons, a grandmother to two grown grandchildren, and a step-grandmother to eighteen.

As one of Oregon's most beloved, respected, and sought-after leaders in the state's Democratic party, Roberts continues to mentor and advise others as they seek leadership positions.

BARBARA ROBERTS FAMILY COLLECTION

Governor Roberts' family celebrated with her at a special dinner in March 2006. Sons Mike and Mark, daughter in-law Tammy (on Barbara's left) and grandchildren (from left) Kaitlin, Melissa, and Robert.

Portland State
UNIVERSITY

The Barbara Roberts Collection

Portland State University Library Special Collections is the proud steward of the Governor Barbara Roberts Papers, an extensive collection of manuscripts, correspondence, drafts of speeches, public presentations, press releases, newsletters, photographs, scrapbooks, clippings, recordings, and other resources related to Governor Roberts's life and career.

As a complement to her official papers held by the Oregon State Archives, Governor Roberts's personal papers offer insight into the political and personal challenges she faced throughout her career as a public servant and the causes she continues to advocate for, including: women's representation in politics and the public sector; equitable education for children on the autism spectrum; civil rights and protections for sexual and gender minority communities; compassionate end-of-life care; and environmental stewardship.

Notable highlights of the collection include recorded public appearances provided as streaming video in the *Barbara Roberts Video Gallery* in Portland State University's digital repository at https://pdxscholar.library.pdx.edu/womenoregon_robertsvideo/

The Video Gallery includes debates from Barbara Roberts's political candidacies; official state speeches, including her inaugurations as Secretary of State and Governor; press conferences; and talks with civil rights organizations, industries, caregivers, and parents. This video collection also includes the most extraordinary "Conversation with Oregon," which was a live, television call-in program that lasted several months in which Governor Roberts spoke on-air with thousands of her constituents from every part of the state.

The Barbara Roberts Papers came to Portland State University Library through a partnership with Portland State's Center for Women's Leadership. It is now part of a vibrant archive of political papers from Oregon's trailblazing women leaders, including Governor Roberts's colleagues in public service, Oregon Senator Avel Gordly, the Honorable Justice Betty Roberts, and Portland City Commissioner Gretchen Kafoury.

Portland State University Library Special Collections provides public access to The Barbara Roberts Papers and Video Gallery and other archival collections for research purposes. For more information, please contact: specialcollections@pdx.edu